HAUNTED HAMILTON, OHIO

SHI O'NEILL

Haunted America

Published by Haunted America
A Division of The History Press
Charleston, SC
www.historypress.com

Copyright © 2021 by Shi O'Neill
All rights reserved

First published 2021

ISBN 9781540249104

Library of Congress Control Number: 2021938536

This book is dedicated to my husband and children,
who encourage and support me in all ways.

CONTENTS

PREFACE

You can't become familiar with the ghosts of the present without taking a peek at the citizens and events from the past. This book ties anomalous events, spirit communications and psychic impressions found over the last decades with the history that could possibly validate those strange and inexplicable happenings. It can make for interesting reading and a little bit of head-scratching for nonbelievers. In the Hamilton of today, you can find a mix of psychic investigations, ghost walks and events that focus on the paranormal, and this book will provide you with the information you need to become a part of those activities if your curiosity gets the best of you.

My first encounter with something I would consider paranormal happened the day after Christmas in 1973. It was a strange time weatherwise for December. The temperature was unseasonably warm for winter, in the sixties, and there were severe thunderstorms. Friends and I went to the theater to see the first showing that night of *The Exorcist*. When we got to the theater, power was out in the entire area because of the storm. We went back to my apartment to wait for the midnight show, hoping the power would be back on at the theater by then. To pass the time, we made a Ouija board out of pieces of paper with the letters of the alphabet and Yes/No written on them. We overturned a wine glass and asked questions while the six of us each held a finger lightly on the glass. Overall, we weren't very successful, and the glass didn't move much as we sat around the table hoping something would happen. It was silly, really. When it was my turn, I asked my question silently because I felt a little ridiculous. My question was "Is my spirit guide here with me?" The wording may have been a little different because in those days I'm sure I wouldn't have known what a spirit guide was. The overturned wine glass started to shake a little bit, and then suddenly it moved in a circle so quickly that everyone's fingers fell away except mine. I could barely hang on. It moved around the table and stopped at Yes. I didn't move the glass and no one else was touching the glass. It made a lasting impression on me. But it didn't make me believe in spirits—angels maybe, but not ghosts.

Personally, I never thought I would ever believe in ghosts. And I really had no interest in local history or history in general until we moved into a six-thousand-square-foot mansion in an area known as Millionaire's Row at the turn of the twentieth century. Now it is merely known as the Dayton Lane Historic District—no millionaires here that I know of. After living in this house for over twenty-five years, I have had a change of heart about ghosts and hauntings. One firsthand experience is all it takes to make you doubt yourself. By researching what could possibly have caused the strange things that happen when you live in an old house, I have taken a keen interest in the history of my house, neighborhood and city.

The chapter titled "The Trial of the Century" recounts real-life unadulterated stories of unusual things that have happened in our home for many years. In the beginning, the encounters were terrifying, and now they have become accepted as normal. Except for frightening our animals and sometimes our children, there honestly have been no issues with living with a few ghosts.

Many of the communications and impressions in this book were supplied by renowned spiritual consultant Victor Paruta, a nationally recognized psychic medium. Victor is the founder and executive director of Cincinnati's Victory of Light Expo, one of the Midwest's largest Body, Mind and Spirit events. He teaches classes in psychic development, ghosts and hauntings and a number of other metaphysical topics. As a popular radio and television personality, he was featured nationally on ABC's *The View* as an expert on ghosts and hauntings and internationally on George Noory's *Beyond Belief* on Gaia TV. Victor has become a great friend to the residents of the Dayton Lane Historic District over the years. This book is not about Victor; however, he has been instrumental in providing many of the communications and impressions presented in this book later verified by research conducted by Dayton Lane residents. TriOPS Paranormal Research and Spiritual Realm Paranormal Investigators provided considerable information resulting from investigations into some of the other unexplained happenings around town. This book is not an endorsement for any of these organizations but merely presents their findings.

So, are you a believer in the paranormal? Do you believe that our essence goes on to another existence beyond this world? For millennia, people have held this belief. Things that we once called superstition or folklore are now proven by science. As Shakespeare's Hamlet attests, "There are more things in heaven and earth, Horatio, than are dreamt in our philosophy." As science fiction daily stuns us as it translates into science, who are we to say that things and people don't exist beyond our limited three dimensions?

Before his death, Abraham Lincoln, so the story goes, saw himself lying dead in a coffin in the White House. And soon after World War II, when Winston Churchill was staying at the White House, he had an unnerving experience. After a long bath with a scotch and cigar, he walked into the next room and was met by the ghost of Abraham Lincoln. Churchill addressed the spirit: "Good evening, Mr. President. You seem to have me at a disadvantage." The spirit smiled and vanished.

Winston Churchill was in good company. Sir Arthur Conan Doyle, author and creator of the ever-popular Sherlock Holmes, spoke to ghosts through mediums. Alan Turing, widely considered to be the father of theoretical computer science and artificial intelligence, believed in telepathy. All these men are known for their genius, but they believed in the impossible. According to analysis, as many as three-quarters of Americans believe in the paranormal in some form, and nearly one in five has actually seen a ghost. Where do you fall in that spectrum?

The intention of this book is to describe paranormal encounters as told by people who experienced them. It presents corroborating history as a potential explanation for sometimes unbelievable phenomena. And if you have any interest in pursuing the mysterious and supernatural yourself, this book will provide some details about where you can get personally involved.

ACKNOWLEDGEMENTS

M y heartfelt thanks to all the people, living and dead, who have contributed to the content of this book. Their contributions, ranging from support and encouragement to the sharing of personal stories, are appreciated and made this publication possible. No one encourages and supports me more than my wonderful husband and family, for they have always believed in me. Also let me thank my editor, John Rodrigue, for having the patience to walk me through this process.

Many people have influenced me and developed my love of history, old houses and with that the strange things that often show up in those old houses. At the top of the list would have to be Sherry Corbett and Bob Sherwin, who began the renaissance in my beautiful historic community. Although both of them have passed on, their presence is forever felt.

Equally important are the following contributors: Dr. Tom Nye, for photos and information about the Dayton Lane Ghost Walk; Jennifer Albinus, for her time spent at the library gathering information and for her generous involvement on the Dayton Lane Board through the years; Jackie Phillips, for sharing her haunting experiences at the Christian Benninghofen House; Chris Carroll, for being the voice of reason grounding me in reality and providing history on her Benninghofen ancestors; Lynne Bell, for information about the paranormal investigations at Ryan's Tavern; and Hannah Faulkner, for allowing me to use her beautiful photo of the Butler County Courthouse.

Acknowledgements

A special thank-you to Kathy Creighton, who spent an entire afternoon giving me a personal tour, including the background of the ghosts, at the Butler County Historical Society and providing the photos and material to expand my knowledge of the history and hauntings of Hamilton. Finally, thanks to my friend of many years Victor Paruta, who challenged the skeptic in me, piquing my interest in the paranormal and helping me understand that not everything can be explained and unseen things can be real.

INTRODUCTION

I f you walk the streets of Hamilton, Ohio, today you will be immersed in the historic charm of small-town America. You will pass sculptures, murals and gorgeous pocket parks at every turn; after all, Hamilton is now known as the "City of Sculpture" and a city of the arts. But it was not always so—in fact, the opposite was true. Hamilton was a blue-collar manufacturing town, providing many industrial jobs that beckoned to Kentuckians looking for work who then migrated north to the paper and steel mills. It was the influential industrialists who built and occupied many of the mansions that still stand in the historic districts. Welcome to Hamilton, located just twenty miles north of Cincinnati in the southwest corner of Ohio.

Spiritualism as a movement didn't appear until 1848, but that doesn't mean that spirit communication didn't exist at the founding of the original fort and establishment of Hamilton as a city. The indigenous people of the time, the Miami tribes, had their own sacred culture. Their religion centered on their attempts to gain power from spirits known as manitous. They believed these spirits roamed the world and could take the form of humans and animals. It was central to their culture to try to contact one of these spirits, or manitou, in a dream by secluding themselves and fasting in order to find their guardian spirit. Men and women both engaged in this practice. Shamans were considered closer than ordinary people to the spirits and would gain power to either heal or kill. They showed their spiritual strength by throwing charmed objects at their enemies and trying to bring the dead back to life.

This Alexander Hamilton sculpture commissioned in 2004 was created by Kristen Visbal. Titled *The American Cape*, it stands over twelve feet tall. *Author's collection.*

A Pioneer Family represents the Stewart family, who arrived in 1802. It is located near the Log House in Monument Park, next to the river. *Author's collection.*

The Miami Indians believed that when someone dies they enter another world, where they walk down a road. The dead are tempted as they make the walk, and they encounter several obstacles that they must overcome before they get to the Beautiful Country. Here there is great abundance and happiness.

This city was originally a frontier fort established in September 1791 along the banks of the Great Miami River and among the Miami Indians, Algonquian people. Fort Hamilton was intended to supply troops for General St. Clair's forays into the Northwest Territories. Living along the frontier in the eighteenth century meant you were subject to attack, and it was St. Clair's responsibility to quell the Native Americans responsible for those attacks. The fort was named for Alexander Hamilton, who was then America's first treasury secretary. When General St. Clair was defeated in Darke County, his troops retreated to Fort Hamilton after significant loss of life. General Anthony Wayne took command of the U.S. Army, and his victory at the Battle of Fallen Timbers finally ended the longstanding land dispute between the United States and the Northwest Indian Confederation over what is now known as Ohio. Many soldiers returned to Fort Hamilton

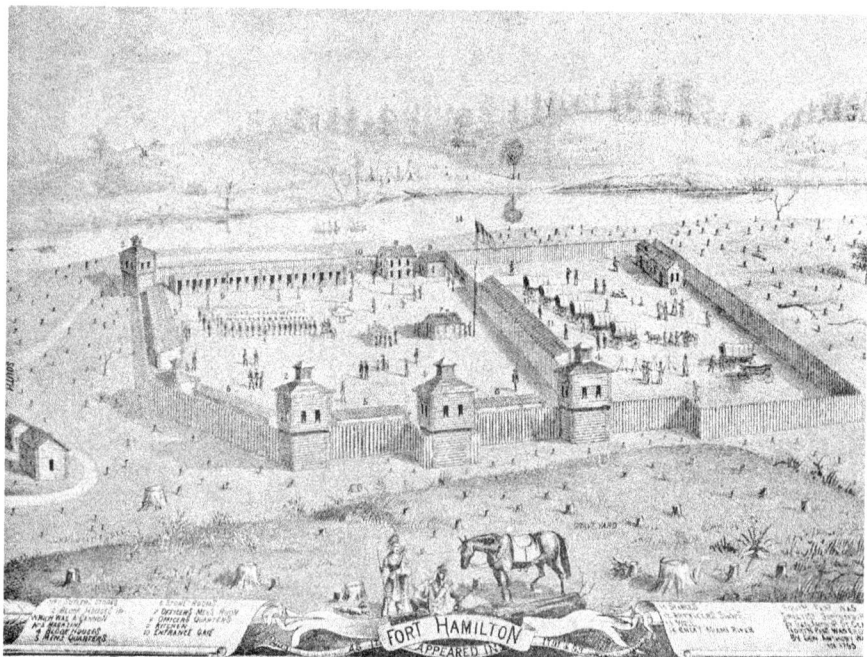

Map of Fort Hamilton, built in 1791 along the banks of the Great Miami River to supply troops for General St. Clair. *Centennial Anniversary of the City of Hamilton Ohio.*

to build permanent homes when General Wayne's army was disbanded. In 1795, a mere three years after it was built, the fort was abandoned. By then, houses were springing up all around the fort and a town was forming, known at that time as Fairfield.

Hamilton had its issues at the start. Originally located only on the east side of the Great Miami River, Hamilton was incorporated in 1810. Five years later, the settlers lost that status because they were not holding proper elections. On the opposite side of the river, the city of Rossville was growing at the same time, and in 1827 Hamilton tried incorporating again, this time with neighboring Rossville. That attempt also failed, lasting only four years. The two cities grew independently, separated by the river. Finally, in 1855, Rossville and Hamilton were successful in their attempt to merge and agreed on the name Hamilton.

While Hamilton and Rossville were trying their best to form a unified city, five hundred miles away in New York the birth of modern Spiritualism in America was taking place. This movement emerged in 1848 when John Fox, his wife and six children moved into their new home. When they heard rapping noises that just couldn't be explained, John's two daughters Maggie and Kate would clap or snap their fingers, doing their best to encourage a rapping response. It worked! Using this method, they were able to communicate with the invisible spirit and learned that he was a peddler who was murdered and buried in their basement. The Spiritualism movement exploded in America once word got out about what was happening in the Fox home. In those days, talking to spirits was considered demonic. The girls were forced to recant their story. but later they admitted that they were telling the truth and became active members of the Spiritualist movement. Spiritualism was popular as a form of entertainment but also as a comfort to those who needed to believe in an afterlife. In 1882, the Society for Psychical Research was founded to examine paranormal phenomena using rigorous, unbiased scientific methods of investigation. They examined the belief in spirit and the ability to connect with them in various ways. It is uncertain how prevalent Spiritualism was in Hamilton at the time of the Industrial Revolution, but there is evidence that it was practiced by some.

By the time the manufacturing age reached America in the 1830s and '40s, Hamilton, Ohio's many attributes contributed to its reputation as a significant industrial town. Cheap labor, the waterpower provided by the Great Miami River and the system of hydraulic canals were advantageous for the development of industries that prompted steady growth for the city. Paper manufacturing and iron production found their way to Hamilton. Well into the twentieth century, Hamilton was known as a manufacturing and industrial center. Due to the prosperity that these industries provided, many Chicago mobsters were lured to the city, bringing illegal gambling and prostitution, and during Prohibition they supported Hamilton's rumrunners and speakeasies. Hamilton was an active gambling community propped up by the sex trade and alcohol. It was during the uproarious times of the 1920s and early 1930s that Hamilton earned its nickname Little Chicago. And believe it or not, some of these racketeers are still hanging around, in spirit, making their presence known to a new generation.

Hamilton takes pride in its four designated historic districts—Downtown Hamilton, Dayton Lane, German Village and Rossville. They were populated by affluent industrialists, businessmen and the laborers who worked for them.

Downtown Hamilton evolved from liveries, small grocers, haberdashers, saloons and theaters. In the twentieth century, the population wanted to change that look to something more modern, so they covered up the lovely early architecture with steel façades to give the city a contemporary look. Now, in the twenty-first century, the false coverings are coming down, exposing those beautiful old buildings, and the downtown area once more has a small-town feel of boutiques, restaurants and entrepreneurs, with every attempt being made to restore the historical look of the city's origins. Those plain coverings that once were thought to give the city a flair of modernization, now gone, reveal exquisite edifices carefully created by early Hamilton craftsmen.

Perched high above the Soldiers and Sailors Monument, located at the site of the old Fort Hamilton next to the High-Main Bridge, Billy Yank has been keeping his eyes and ears on the city of Hamilton since 1904. This beautiful sculpture of a Union foot soldier is the creation of Rudolph Theim, a local artist. The monument that it crowns is a tribute to soldiers playing a part in all our country's wars, starting with the Civil War. The artifacts and stories in this somber place make one feel that only a whisper is appropriate as you walk among the hallowed rooms, out of respect to those lost and represented here.

The Dayton Lane Historic District was known as Millionaire's Row and home to many prominent businessmen. A stroll through the neighborhood will reveal a true community, where neighbors help neighbors and talk over fences, a place where residents care about each other. It includes the beautiful four-block Campbell Avenue Park that separates the houses on the north and south sides of Campbell Avenue. At the urging of Robert C. McKinney to give the public a park, what began as a racetrack was donated to the city by Lewis D. Campbell, who was a well-known representative to Congress for the state of Ohio and also served as a minister to Mexico. The park has been restored by the city and is lovingly cared for by residents of the Dayton Lane district. A walk through the park at dusk can overcome you with the feeling of days long ago, and you can easily imagine you are walking with the spirits of times past.

Rossville was known throughout the 1800s for its inns, agricultural businesses and breweries. Main Street is the main thoroughfare through that part of town and is lined with beautiful nineteenth-century commercial buildings. At the dawn of the twentieth century you would have found taverns, stables, hatters, meeting halls, drugstores and grocers. The district retains the name of the early city that grew along the west side of the Great Miami River. In addition to the eclectic Main Street area, the district has beautiful old homes surrounded by the smaller homes of the working class.

Rossville has its share of urban legends based on tragic incidents from long ago. In 1833, a cholera epidemic took the life of a bride-to-be of the westside community. In 1833, what is now known as Wayne Park—where

Billy Yank is a sculpture of a Union foot soldier that crowns the Soldiers and Sailors Monument located next to the Great Miami River *Author's collection.*

children play on the seesaw, swings and slides—was a cemetery. The young woman who should have been walking down the aisle to meet her betrothed was sadly buried on her wedding day in the cemetery between present-day Park Avenue, Wayne Avenue and North D Street. The devastated groom was found lying dead on her grave a few days later, the victim of a self-inflicted bullet. For decades, those who traveled in and around the Rossville Cemetery reported seeing their ghosts dancing through the headstones.

Not far from the cemetery there used to be a church at the southwest corner of South A and Arch Streets, near the stone arched viaduct carrying trains across the Great Miami River. The story goes that the ghost of a headless woman was said to haunt that church. If there is a kernel of truth to this legend, it can't be found today. No church exists at this location, only a grassy strip that runs along the river. Did a church ever sit there? Who was the woman, and what was her story? Only the urban legend remains.

Like Rossville, the German Village Historic District is a mix of lovely homes and commercial enterprises. It is located immediately north of Hamilton's central business district and lies adjacent to the Great Miami River. This area was the first residential development outside of Fort Hamilton housing both prominent businessmen and laborers, as illustrated by the variety of architectural styles. With all the riverfront development spurred on by the arrival of the Spooky Nook Sports Complex, German Village welcomes a gentrification of its own. Beautiful old homes are being restored, restaurants and boutique businesses are moving in and the atmosphere is electrifying. It is in German Village that you'll find the Butler County Historical Society and its hosts of ghosts roaming the building.

It seems that Spiritualism began to wan midcentury and later in the twentieth century, although you can still find a Spiritualist church if you have a mind to. Instead, paranormal offerings manifest in the form of fortune-tellers, palm readers and psychics. By the last half of the century, you could walk into a corner storefront or a strip mall and get your fortune told through tarot cards, palm reading or even by reading the lumps on your head. Needless to say, many of these were merely a way of making a living and not scientific or credible in any way. But then there was Edgar Cayce, an uneducated clairvoyant and trance medium from Hopkinsville, Kentucky. He was a deeply religious man who thought that he was channeling his higher self. He gave credibility to the paranormal field and was nicknamed the "Sleeping Prophet." Many believable prophets and clairvoyants came along in the twentieth century—not all were false. Beliefs in otherworldly phenomena were becoming more acceptable, and it was less traumatic for you to see a psychic. Many were, and are, looking for the comfort and hope that better times are ahead.

Toward the end of the twentieth century, changes in business and industry caused widespread job loss in the city of Hamilton. The city struggled as business left the downtown areas and Hamilton slowly lost the manufacturing giants that once brought jobs and prosperity. It was left with only the phantoms of days past in the form of abandoned factories and smokestacks. It was a difficult time for Hamilton, and many years passed with a downtown that looked more like a ghost town. The need arose for the city to find a new identity.

The dawn of the twenty-first century found the town reinventing itself as a center of art and sculpture. The Fitton Center, founded in 1993 by Donald Fitton Jr. and Claire Fitton, who were generous patrons of the arts, brought music, dance, theater and art to the heart of the city. Hamilton was in the beginning stages of a renaissance that changed the focus from manufacturing to service industries, entertainment and entrepreneurial enterprises. Shortly after the Fitton Center made its debut along the beautiful riverfront, the Pyramid Hill Sculpture Park and Museum was established, and in the summer of 2000, Hamilton was officially recognized as the City of Sculpture. In the years that followed there has been a revitalization of the downtown areas on both sides of the river. And now the river provides a place for entertainment with the Rivers Edge Amphitheater, on the perimeter of German Village, as a popular concert venue. The Great Miami rowing teams can be seen slicing their way through the currents, and the Spooky Nook Sports Complex, overlooking the river, will bring jobs of a different sort to the city whose manufacturing days seem to be over.

The citizens of Hamilton in the nineteenth century weren't overtly curious about the paranormal, nor was it an accepted belief in the Midwest at that time. That's not to say that stranger-than-fiction things didn't happen, it's just that they weren't talked about. There were haunted houses at Halloween and scary stories of course, but no one took it seriously, not in Hamilton. In 2003, a group of neighbors in Dayton Lane sat around a firepit. It was springtime, not even Halloween when people bring out their scary tales. But around the fire, real tales of extraordinary events happening in some of the houses became the topic of conversation. That single occasion was the impetus for a fundraiser for the district named the Ghost Walk of Dayton Lane. That was the first organized, publicized and factual exploration into the paranormal. The ghost walk has been presented every year since then. Other areas of town followed suit and started their own paranormal investigations, bringing in a variety of ghost hunters and paranormal investigators. It wasn't something to be made fun of anymore, and it is surprising just how many people have had their own experiences and are believers.

With all the physical and cultural changes occurring over the centuries, Hamilton continues to respect and maintain its historic neighborhoods, and it has revitalized the downtown with an eye toward the past. This book addresses the industrialists, characters and events from more than one hundred years ago that have helped define the essence of this once again thriving Midwest town. It will explore the spirits that continue to make their presence known in a city that honors its history.

1

THE VORTEX AT McKEE MANOR

L ocated in the Dayton Lane Historic District, the McKee mansion sits at the northwest corner of Seventh and Dayton Streets. When Victor Paruta walked through McKee Manor, a name adopted by the current owners, he had no prior knowledge of the house or its history. In fact, he wanted no information on any of the homes he toured so he could read the homes without influence.

John McKee was a Civil War captain who was seriously wounded at the Battle of Stones River, one of the deadliest battles of the war with twenty-three thousand casualties in total, North and South.

John married his wife, Sarah Beckett, the daughter of a prominent Hamilton businessman, in 1861, just a short time before leaving for the war. Unfortunately, John came back from the war seriously wounded. When he returned home, John took a teaching position to support his growing family. Once reunited, Sarah gave birth to two young daughters and a little boy. Sadly, their son didn't survive to see his first birthday. Sarah's mother, Mary Beckett, lived with them in her final years until she died in 1873. After teaching, John became the postmaster general for the city of Hamilton, and he built this lovely corner home at Seventh and Dayton Streets for his family.

In McKee Manor, Victor discovered the spirits of a man and a woman who still reside there. The supposition was that it is the original owners, Captain John McKee and his wife, Sarah.

Outside the house, watching over the two spirits inside, is the ghost of an older woman, Sarah's mother perhaps? She peers through the window

Left: John McKee, Civil War captain who was seriously wounded at the Battle of Stones River and a postmaster for the city of Hamilton. *Author's collection.*

Right: Sarah McKee was wife to Captain John McKee, who was wounded in the Civil War. *Author's collection.*

as though spying on the couple. The impression of the older woman was someone who was pretentious or condescending. Since Sarah was born a Beckett, an influential family in the city of Hamilton, is it possible that the ghost is her mother, Mary?

Now, it is true that John McKee was a Civil War captain, but there is another captain associated with this great old mansion. At some point, McKee Manor was converted to apartments or used as a boardinghouse, so many people passed through over the years. Victor sensed a young sea captain, a man who was tall and had an outgoing personality. This captain was a handsome figure of a man, and oh how he loved to tell stories. He had traveled around the world and seen many things, so he had lots of stories about strange customs and faraway places to tell anyone who would listen. Unlike many of the other spirits who swirl through this vortex, he enjoys interacting with people. If you find yourself on this corner in the quiet of the night, you just might hear the strains of a sea chantey floating faintly in the air.

Years after Victor Paruta visited the house, a former resident of Dayton Lane, who grew up less than a block from McKee Manor in the 1920s, made some casual comments about the house while he visited the

Home built for John and Sarah McKee, located in the Dayton Lane Historic District. *Author's collection.*

neighborhood. He had no knowledge of Victor's tour and assessment. He mentioned that one of his boyhood memories was of an old sailor who lived in this home. The old man was not too friendly to the area children. He was reclusive and spent much of his time drinking alone. Could the spirit of the storytelling captain be a younger version of the old drunken sailor? Or is this just a coincidence?

Many things have happened over the years that have caused this historic community to believe that the McKee mansion is haunted. Occupants of this house have reported lights turning on and off for no apparent reason, furniture being moved and clothing inexplicably coming off wall hooks. Another strange recent incident involves a young boy who lived in the house. This child was seemingly "locked" in one of the many rooms of this three-story home. His parents tried with all their might to open the door. They couldn't understand why it wouldn't budge because there was no lock on the door, yet they were unable to pry it open. While they took a break to plan their next move, the door mysteriously opened on its own. The child was free. It is possible the door was swollen or jammed, but two adults were unable to force the door open. That hardly makes sense. The young boy lacked the strength to help his situation—how did the heavy old wooden door open on its own?

The house was long ago converted to apartments, and recently, one of the tenants insisted that she firmly latched a door in her apartment only to have it open on its own. This happened on a regular basis. Frustrated, she now no longer latches the door; she just leaves it open to avoid dealing with the baffling mystery.

Taking the back stairs up to the next level of this three-story house, Victor spoke about a different feeling overcoming him as he approached the second floor. There are four ghosts in the second-floor apartments. "I feel a penny-pinching male, much older and not outgoing at all, he always kept to himself." Second, he sensed a thick and strong energy, uncomfortable like someone who eats too much or maybe has a heart problem.

A third ghost was someone who was dragged up the steps. Victor said, "He's not strong or healthy. He has a peculiar outlook and a set of priorities that are different from other people. He doesn't want to be bothered by things that might be important to other people." This ghost was described as having a mental abnormality. He is sad and heavy, heavy in the heart. He is not a balanced person mentally or emotionally. And the last spirit is an elderly man, alone in his own world. He didn't like or want visitors.

What a depressing reading for the ghosts on the second floor of this beautiful Victorian mansion—what could be going on here? What was Victor tuning into? Around 1931, McKee Manor was the Community Home for the Aged and provided care for convalescents and invalids in nicely furnished rooms. Before her death, Belle Davis Andrews, widow of Allen Andrews, a prominent member of the Butler County Bar, turned their home into a place for those with infirmities. She loved to tell the story about her childhood when she came by covered wagon to Ohio. In September 1937, her obituary in the *Hamilton Daily News Journal* noted that "Mrs. Andrews often told of the long journey in a covered wagon from Iowa to Ohio." Victor found a Victorian lady spirit on the back steps that could well have been Mrs. Andrews, who lived in the house from at least 1901 until her death in 1937.

There is only one traffic light in the Dayton Lane Historic District, located at Seventh and Dayton Streets. It's a dangerous spot for traffic traveling through the neighborhood. For some reason, many accidents occur at this corner, and it is one of the most psychically active areas in the city. It has often been described by locals and visitors as the "passageway to the other side." Spirits flow freely between the McKee mansion and Heaven on 7th on the opposite corner, sometimes with frightful results.

2

HEAVEN ON 7TH

U ndoubtedly, the most frightening area in Dayton Lane is the corner
of Seventh and Dayton Streets. It was described by Victor Paruta
as a spiritual vortex with souls moving from what used to be Major
John Bender's house through a portal on the third floor to the house diagonal,
known as the McKee mansion. Major Bender was a well-regarded builder and
community leader. John McKee was the postmaster general who occupied the
house on the opposite corner in the nineteenth century. The Bender Mansion,
though originally a single-family home, was later known to have been a
boardinghouse and a lawyer's office, and at the time Victor toured the house,
it was a massage parlor and day spa known as Heaven on 7th.

The hauntings at Heaven on 7th came to the Dayton Lane Board's
attention when the masseuses told some of the board members about
poltergeist activity involving a pie safe. (A pie safe is a piece of furniture
designed to store pies and other food items. This was a normal household
item before iceboxes came into regular use, and it was an important part of
the American household from the 1700s through the 1800s.) Located on
the first floor in the spa area, it would open on its own for some unknown
reason. The staff members would close it and leave the empty room, and
when they returned it was open again. It was a snug fit, so a mechanical
failure was not a possibility. The two employees agreed that this was a near
daily occurrence.

An interesting side note, other than the Heaven on 7th massage and day spa,
this building was also occupied by a therapeutic massage therapist in 1938. As
Victor always says, "Spirits in a home often attract like-minded people."

Civil War major John Bender's house, at one time known as Heaven on 7th, located at Seventh and Dayton Streets in Dayton Lane Historic District. *Author's collection.*

On the night that Victor toured Heaven on 7th, he was followed by a team who took notes, videotaped the event and followed closely with a tape recorder. The idea was that with three people documenting what happened, nothing should be missed. Victor sensed up to forty different ghosts moving back and forth between the Bender and McKee mansions that made up the vortex, but they were transient and merely moving through the house. He didn't feel that they were evil. The spirits appeared to be from different periods; there was what was described as a "Gibson Girl" and another from what appeared to be a 1930s timeframe. There was a rugged-looking man in a white T-shirt and a newsboy cap.

This tour was different from the others because there were several people other than the three documenters who followed behind. When the group got to the third-floor hallway, several strange things occurred. For one, there was a heavy sense of dread, to the point that some were fighting tears. The group of followers became antagonistic and started arguing and were made to stop so the psychic had quiet to carry out his work. Located in the back of the top floor were two plain rooms and a small kitchen. Victor sensed bad vibrations and felt sickness and death overcoming a small child. In this apartment, he found a tall, thin man in a long coat, apparently a boat captain, who was the cause of most of the poltergeist activity. The cadre of documenters encountered the small entourage in the hallway, and feelings of hostility again overtook the atmosphere. The entire evening was one of bad vibrations.

After the visit to Heaven on 7th, one of those attending awoke the same night between two and three o'clock in the morning with a burning pain in the abdomen. On inspection, beneath the pajama bottoms were three bloody claw marks spanning the width of the stomach. It caused confusion because they were too deep for nail scratches, and they looked like animal claw marks. It didn't make sense. A similar event happened to one of the guides on the Dayton Lane Ghost Walk. He returned home after taking his group to Heaven on 7th, and when he removed his suit jacket and silk shirt, he found the same three bloody claw marks on his arm. In both cases, there was no evidence of the marks on the clothing. In both cases, in a matter of hours all signs of the bloody scratches had disappeared. Some say such marks come from demons and a prayer of protection should be said. This group wasn't in the habit of offering prayers of protection. And there are others who say that spirits can't physically harm anyone in the corporeal world. The fact remains, the marks were there.

How do you explain the events of those nights? Why were so many spirits in that particular location? It is known that the Bender mansion was a boardinghouse with as many as eighteen rooms rented out at one time. The main intersection at Seventh and Dayton was supposedly on the trolley route with a stop at this corner. Perhaps the spirits are still getting on and off the trolley.

And what about the strange behavior in the top-floor hallway? In the nineteenth and early twentieth centuries, most people died in their homes, and this large mansion was no exception. Deaths occurred for a variety of reasons, not only old age but also the influenza epidemic, among other causes. Bodies were laid out in the home in those days, so it's not surprising that our psychic sensed, with great pain, a young person passing into death on the third floor. The feeling of dread and anxiety by those in attendance, along with the toxic atmosphere, were oppressive to all involved.

A tenant who lived on the second floor at the time Victor toured the house illustrated a perfect example of the concept that although some spirits are tied to a house, others are attached to certain people. This tenant had the spirits of her departed parents with her. She was physically dragged out of her bed. Victor sensed two ghosts in her bedroom, a tall male with a round head and a female. They were positive but strong energies. The woman was walking around cleaning things up, and she wanted to make the bed, so she pulled the tenant out of the bed along with the covers. The female occupant would wake up in the middle of the night and see red eyes shining in the dark of the bedroom along with flashing white lights. She saw the manifestation of a man wearing a long black coat and could hear people talking. Sometimes, furniture in her bedroom moved, maybe it was her mother cleaning? All these physical manifestations would indicate poltergeist activity. One night she heard tapping on the walls, and the chandelier started to swing before falling on her head.

Victor peered out the bedroom window and commented, "A whole group of spirits are gathering outside the house. This house is a revolving door vortex as spirits pass through."

Another person who lived in the house in the late 1990s reported that a handsome male ghost with a mischievous spirit lived in her apartment. She was a writer and called him her "muse." Kitchen chairs would move without warning, and sometimes she could feel his penetrating eyes staring back at her from across the room. She could hear him singing while she was in the shower, and he occasionally rattled the pots and pans. The tenant felt no fear—in fact, she looked forward to his attentions.

Many impressions came to Victor that later were validated by either research at the library or independent firsthand accounts. One striking example was his sense of a large Black woman, her hair tied up in a kerchief and sporting an apron. She was standing in the kitchen peering out the back door and a good cook who spent a lot of time in the kitchen. The next year during a ghost walk tour it so happened that a friend of the furniture movers who had helped the massage parlor move in was on the tour. They commented to the tour guide that this was the house where the movers saw a Black woman scrubbing floors on the second floor as they carried items into the house. They even commented that she looked like Aunt Jemima. When the movers mentioned it to the employees of the massage parlor, they were told that there was no one else in the building. The information about Victor's impression of a female spirit in the kitchen had been omitted from the tour since it wasn't verified, so the men couldn't have known about the spirit from the tour commentary.

Of all the houses Victor "read" for us, Heaven on 7th housed more spirits and impressions than any of the others. Among the preponderance of otherworldly souls encountered, there were multiple people who were sick and/or died in the house. The masseuses who worked there said the male ghost materialized when he opened the pie safes. There was a heavyset Black woman who worked in the kitchen, a delivery man in a beret, Gibson girls, an attractive couple who ran the house and angels in the kitchen. There appeared to be a slender old woman who was so sad that she was inconsolable. She had lost someone in a war and then lost her inheritance to someone she trusted to manage her finances who stole everything she had. In the house there was a Victorian female music teacher and another woman with a name sounding like "Bella." Bella was probably a chambermaid who experienced death in the house. Many more were present during that investigative tour, too many to list. You can get an idea of just how crowded with spirits this house is.

All these hauntings occurred while the lovely three-story mansion was occupied by the massage parlor/day spa and multiple tenants of the various apartments. Later, the house was sold to a lovely couple who turned it into a single-family home. They made massive changes, updating the house and bringing light and positive energy to the building. They didn't believe in hauntings, and after they moved in with their young children, the spirits moved out. Maybe they no longer felt welcome—or just maybe they passed through the vortex to a more appropriate location.

3

THE CRYING BOY

Nothing is more incredible than hearing of a haunting from a die-hard skeptic who now doubts his skepticism. This was the case of two network technicians who crawled through the bowels of a century-plus-year-old house, pulling and testing cable as they went from drop to drop.

"David, do you hear that? Over."

"Are you talking about the crying? I do. Over."

"Let's change the channel. Go to channel 8. Over."

"OK, are you there now? Over."

"I'm with you, but I still hear the crying. Over."

"How can that be? First of all, we're underground so we couldn't be picking up a baby monitor. How are we hearing this? Over."

"I don't know, switch to channel 15. Over."

"I'm there now, can you hear me? Over."

"I can, but it doesn't seem we can get rid of this crying child. Let's just get our work done and get out of here."

"Over."

This is a conversation that undeniably occurred and is a firsthand account. What makes this encounter extraordinary is that it was experienced by two people simultaneously. It wasn't a product of anyone's overactive imagination.

While the techs were running a network cable in a basement, a child's crying could be heard in their two-way radio headsets. The location was in the crawlspace behind the furnace room. Two contractors were running network cables in Nye Family Vision when the optometry practice moved to 712 Dayton Street in Historic Dayton Lane.

Like many of the homes in the Dayton Lane District, the history behind this grand old home is significant. As with other homes in the district, the stories came before the research that uncovered the history. The information came not only from descendants who still live in the area but also from news accounts that can be accessed through ancestry.com and newspapers.com.

Asa Shuler was a carpenter who sought his fortune in the gold fields of California in the mid-nineteenth century. After only a few years, he returned home, resuming his life as a carpenter until he founded the Shuler & Benninghofen Woolen Mills with partner John Benninghofen. It was Asa's son, William Asa Shuler, and his wife, Luella May, who took great care in constructing this three-story 8,200-square-foot Prairie-style home in 1910. William bought the property where his house now stands in 1902, removed the existing structure and then built this lovely home. Its exterior brick was fired in Belgium and arrived individually paper wrapped. The spacious interior features quartered oak molding, a beautiful Rookwood fireplace and a solid mahogany beamed ceiling. William chose this particular location for his home because the streetcar ran directly from Seventh and Dayton to

Prairie-style home built in 1910 by William Asa Shuler, of Shuler and Benninghofen, and his wife, Luella May. *Author's collection.*

his woolen mill in Lindenwald. It sounds like such a lovely home, but it is occupied by more than its corporeal inhabitants.

In 1931, poor Luella May Shuler broke her ankle getting into her car, making it near impossible to get around this large three-story house with all its stairs. After her accident, she had a difficult time maneuvering the steps to the upper floors, so an elevator was installed. Luella May died in 1944 of a heart attack at the advanced age of eighty-one, but she was still a vibrant and active woman. Her husband, William, died six years earlier. The home remained in the family until 1950.

The Shuler mansion has a great history, and it also has its share of ghostly tales. Probably the most shocking is the mystery of the crying boy. Who was he? There are a couple possibilities. An 1894 *Republican* news article recounts the story of "horrendous luck" for William Shuler's son. Poor little Frank Shuler, son of William and grandson to Asa, narrowly escaped death when a folding bed collapsed on him. But the unfortunate events didn't end there. Only a few days later, he was climbing on his grandfather's fence, as playful young boys sometimes will, and disastrously fell. Young Frank narrowly escaped impalement on the spiked wrought-iron rail, a dangerous and painful accident that left him seriously ill.

IMPALED ON A FENCE
Frank Shuler Meets with a Painful and Serious Accident—A Young Boy's Mishap

Frank Shuler, the young son of William Shuler, of the Third ward, seems to be peculiarly unfortunate in the matter of accidents. It will be remembered that a few nights since he had a narrow escape from death by the collapse of a folding bed, and now he is seriously ill as the result of a dangerous and painful accident that occurred Tuesday evening while paying a short visit to his grandfather, Asa Schuler on North Third street. Boy-like he was playing about the fences. While attempting to climb over the side fence, he fell and struck on the iron front fence narrowly escaped being impaled as it was one of the iron points pierced his clothing and made an awful wound in his abdomen. Medical aid was at once had and the wound sewed up. The boy is now lying at his home seriously ill and the consequences of the accident are greatly feared.

Over one hundred years have passed, but is it possible that the cries that echo through the young boy's home are Frank's?

It was a wrought-iron fence like this one on which Frank Shuler nearly impaled himself in 1894. *Dayton Lane Historic District Archive.*

Another possibility for the cries in the cablers' headsets could come from the energy of a young boy who was punished in the basement and sensed by Victor Paruta. According to Victor, the young boy was punished by an old man who drank too much and tried to molest young people. The renowned psychic felt the old man took care of horses and was the husband of a laundress. He was a nasty, cruel and critical person, and even though his wife was a good woman, she was never appreciated by him. This communication, or possibly just an imprint, was found behind the furnace room. The fact that the boy's energy was discovered behind the furnace and was heard in the headsets in the crawlspace behind the furnace makes it quite possible that this little spirit is the source for the crying. Was this a real happening? A real ghost? Or just a strong impression of what happened in the basement as felt by a famous psychic? But how does that explain the very real crying heard by two network technicians?

Luella May Shuler was a lovely, well-traveled and sophisticated woman who ran a beautiful house. When Victor toured the three-story home, he felt her presence especially on the third floor. "I think she feels stuck up here, that she is having trouble with her leg and can't walk. But someone picks her up and carries her downstairs because she is unable to manage the steps." He sensed the butler carried her up the backstairs frequently and that he was extremely loyal to Shuler. The current owner of the house confided that the elevator was put in the back of the house due to an injury Luella May suffered when she broke her ankle in the driveway. This implies a certain degree of verification to the story about Mrs. Shuler. Victor felt that the butler ghost was very happy in the house and that he was surrounded by the spirit of his beloved mother who had passed. Once again, there was no mention of Mrs. Shuler or her accident before the house was toured by Victor, which makes his findings somewhat credible.

The optometry office has recently relocated to a restored historic building nearby, and the house is going to be a single-family home again. But at one time, when the building was home to the optometry office, it was also home to an unusual regular occurrence in this very public space. Just ask the staff. Imagine going about your business and someone speaks to you through the intercom on the phone system. Needless to say, the employees were startled and baffled about where the muffled voice came from. On more than one occasion, and witnessed by more than one employee, shadows appeared on the wall when no one else was in the building. This wasn't a case of being scared of one's own shadow.

The optometry office had an ornate waiting room with two lines of chairs separated by a large coffee table. Patients waited there until the doctor or a staff member entered to take them to the back room. One day the doctor entered the waiting room to talk to a patient and her young son who was sitting next to her.

"Have you found the money?" the little boy asked the doctor. "There's money hidden in here somewhere." Now you could just chalk this up to an overactive imagination of a youngster, or you could consider it further validation for the words of a renowned psychic who years earlier said that there was a large sum of money buried somewhere in the house. If the little boy spoke the truth and the psychic impressions are correct, since the house is undergoing restoration now that the optometry offices have moved out, perhaps the money will be found.

4

WILHELMINA AND THE BUTLER COUNTY HISTORICAL SOCIETY

I f you are inclined to have a personal experience with spirit, an excellent place to begin is at the Butler County Historical Society on North Second Street in Hamilton. It is one of the most active of Hamilton's haunted buildings. There you can find a multitude of historical artifacts and, yes, uncanny experiences. The museum was once home to a prominent industrialist, John Benninghofen and his beautiful wife, Wilhelmina, who watches over her home and possessions even today. How do I know this? I spoke to Wilhelmina, a classic Victorian lady and John's second wife, during a visit to the historical society while researching this book.

As you walk in the front door of this exquisite Italianate structure and turn to the left, you enter the drawing room, where Wilhelmina stands guard over her domain. I enjoyed a close-up tour of this room and took a good look at her beautiful sapphire wedding ring—without touching of course, I wouldn't want to offend Wilhelmina.

There are many lovely antiques filling this room, but there are a few special pieces that Wilhelmina is very protective of and calls her own. The best place to look for her is on the ornate gray velvet settee, a focal point in this formal parlor, in the ornately carved matching side chair close by or in the formal dining room down the hall, where a beautifully set table showcases her daughter-in-law's china and Wilhelmina's ivory-handled flatware.

I walked into the room, led by Kathy Creighton, the director of the Butler County Historical Society. Because of the weight of the notebooks and folders that I carried in my arms, I naively thought I would place them on the settee so I could take a closer look at Wilhelmina's wedding ring.

Formal portraits of John Benninghofen (*left*) and his wife, Wilhelmina (*right*), hanging in the Butler County Historical Society. *Author's collection.*

"Oh no, don't sit them there," Kathy warned me.

"I'm sorry," I said, thinking that the furniture in the room was fragile and I should really be more careful.

"Wilhelmina is sitting there," she told me. "You'll find her either on the settee or in this chair next to the fireplace."

"How do you know that?" I asked.

"Well, let's just ask her where she is."

Kathy grasped two copper dowsing rods, one in each hand. I wasn't expecting much but soon changed my mind.

"Wilhelmina, are you sitting on the settee? Cross the rods for yes or move them out if no."

To my surprise, the rods slowly crossed over each other. She handed the rods to me to try.

"Wilhelmina," Kathy said, "Will you speak with Shi who is here with me? Cross the rods if yes."

I held the rods loosely in my hands and unbelievably, without any assistance on my part, the rods crossed. To run a little test, just to make sure that the rods don't cross every time, I asked a question that I thought might get a negative response.

"Wilhelmina, would it be OK if I hold your wedding ring?" Without any hesitation, the rods quickly moved to the outside at a 180-degree angle from

Wilhelmina's ghost often sits on her favorite settee in the drawing room of the Benninghofen House. *Author's collection.*

each other. A definite *no.* Kathy explained that Wilhelmina is very particular about who handles her precious wedding ring, and it is usually hidden behind the flowers on the fireplace mantel.

"You see," Kathy explained, "you don't have to be in darkness to talk to a spirit." As it was proven to me on that day, darkness isn't a necessity.

The Butler County Historical Society has, on many occasions, hosted paranormal investigators as fundraisers for the museum. During those events, which occur after nightfall, they turn out all the lights and use their equipment to try to isolate earthbound spirits. They are looking for cold spots of at least a drop of ten degrees Fahrenheit and might use a MEL meter, which measures both temperature and electromagnetic fields. Often, they'll use an EVP or a digital voice recorder to record sounds that may not be obvious at the time but upon further analysis may provide a response from spirits. In the case of Wilhelmina, she was spotted lying on the floor by an SLS, or Structured Light Sensor camera. This camera supposedly shows a ghost in stick form by projecting an infrared laser grid over a wide area, and any movement, visible or invisible, manifests as a stick

China table setting in the dining room of the Butler County Historical Society, owned by Anna Benninghofen, daughter-in-law to John and Wilhelmina. *Author's collection.*

representation on the camera. Does the camera really show ghosts? There are differing opinions on this subject. Divining rods are a less expensive and more intimate tool, as illustrated that day by Kathy. It seems to be a more personal interaction with spirit.

Kathy shared a fascinating anecdote involving this interesting and "proper" Victorian spirit. She told of a visit from a medium who was getting a tour of the museum. Kathy and this medium entered the dining room as part of the tour, and the antique table was set with china and silver as though ready for a dinner party. At the head of the table, the place setting included Wilhelmina's pearl-handled flatware. There is only one setting of Wilhelmina's silverware available at the museum, and it adorned the place at the head of the table. The medium stopped abruptly and addressed Kathy.

"Kathy, Wilhelmina wants to know if you know how to correctly set a table."

"What? Of course, I do." Kathy replied.

"She said to take another look at the place setting."

Wilhelmina Benninghofen's ivory place setting referred to in a spirit communication. *Author's collection.*

They looked at the setting at the head of the table where Wilhelmina's flatware was displayed, and sure enough, the cutting edge of the knife was facing away from the plate. Kathy corrected the error, and the medium assured her that Wilhelmina was satisfied now.

As was common practice at the time, when Wilhelmina, John and three of their children died, they would have been laid out in the house. It is assumed that she died of a stroke. The cause of death on her death certificate proclaimed she died of paralysis, which was a common term used by coroners at the time for a stroke. One of the mediums familiar with the Historical Society Museum could see her spirit lying flat in the center of the drawing room floor; the significance of that can only be speculated.

Just across the hall, and opposite Wilhelmina's drawing room, is a small but charming library. As you enter the library on the left is a life-sized bust of Brigadier General Ferdinand VanDerVeer. The general was a leader of the Thirty-Fifth Ohio Volunteer Infantry and served during the Civil War. The bust of the general was gifted from his home on South D Street. It greets each visitor as they enter the much smaller space that showcases several

related artifacts, photos and information boards about the celebrated soldier and citizen. On posterboards you can read about the general's life of service in the war and after war to the city of Hamilton. These materials explain that after an outstanding performance at the Battles of Chickamauga and Missionary Ridge, General VanDerVeer returned to a law practice in Hamilton and was later elected judge to the Butler County Court of Common Pleas.

After describing the significance of the library and its various displays, Kathy relaxed and loosely held the copper rods in her hands. She introduced me and asked the general if she could share the details of his life with me as she understood them. After a sign to the affirmative, indicating that he gave his permission, Kathy shared his message. He considered it of great importance that the heroics of his men at Chickamauga were not forgotten, and it is the reason the general keeps residence in the museum. General VanDerVeer wants everyone to know that his biggest fear is that the identity of the Chickamauga Battlefield will be lost to history. The Battle of Chickamauga was the second-costliest battle of the Civil War, ranking only behind Gettysburg. Over sixteen thousand Union soldiers died in that battle, and even though the Confederacy clearly won, the South lost over eighteen thousand men. Kathy respectfully tells the story of Chickamauga and keeps the history and lessons of the Civil War alive.

Leaving the general and the library behind, I followed Kathy up the stairs to the second-floor hallway, a light-hearted area with display cases full of antique dolls and toys. It is here that the giggly spirits of two young girls sit playing in the middle of the floor. I can't say that I saw them, but Kathy hears and communicates with them. I will admit that I felt happy as I passed through the area where they are known to play.

That light-hearted feeling left me when I walked into a bedroom containing the photos and belongings of Hamilton's first mayor, James McBride. I stood quietly between the foot of the bed and his desk listening to the accounts of his spirit interacting with visitors. I was snapping photos of the portraits of the sweet little girls who play in the hall when I was overcome by a coldness

Bust of Civil War brigadier general Ferdinand VanDerVeer. *Author's collection.*

Portrait of James McBride, first mayor for the city of Hamilton. *Author's collection.*

overtaking my back and arms. I not only experienced a chill, but I also had gooseflesh and quietly hid my anxiety. This is not a story or figment of my imagination; it is a factual account of what happened, and the chills were an involuntary response. Kathy questioned McBride with the help of the dowsing rods. As it turns out, he wasn't happy about the intrusion. Not deterred by his response, we stayed in the bedroom for quite a while as Kathy shared what she knew about the lives of McBride, Anna and Isabella. At least I wasn't pushed, just bothered. I've been told that the spirit of James McBride has been known to touch or push people during tours. During one paranormal investigation, he emphatically told the investigators repeatedly to "get out" via the digital voice recorder. As part of that investigation, in order

Kathy Creighton, director of the Butler County Historical Society, talking to James McBride about using dowsing rods. *Author's collection.*

to determine whether it was James McBride who was communicating with the group, he was asked, "Who was the last president that you remember?" The response "Lincoln" could clearly be heard on the recorder. Kathy, who knows her history, insisted that the response was wrong, that McBride died before Lincoln was president. After a bit of fact-checking, she found that James McBride died two weeks after the election that put Lincoln into office. The response on the digital recorder was correct.

Anna and Isabella Owens, the girls who play in the hall, were the daughters of Job Owens of Hooven, Owens, Rentschler Company, which manufactured steam and diesel engines in Hamilton in 1883. The company operated the largest exclusive Corliss engine plant in the country, employing eight hundred workers. Anna and Isabella would certainly have lived lives of privilege. The adult lives of the sisters could not have gone in more opposite directions. Anna grew into a beautiful young lady who earned her degree from Vassar and postgraduate degree from Yale. After her mother's death, Anna went to continue her studies in Paris, where she was a patron of the arts. Poor Isabella died in Columbus at the Home for the Feeble Minded. Very little is known about Isabella's life; however, the federal census shows her as an inmate at the institution from the age of at least forty-one in 1910 until her death. The *Hamilton Evening Democrat* reported in 1906 that she was a defendant in a lawsuit filed by Anna against her and the guardian of Bella's estate after her mother's death. In this filing, she was labeled an "imbecile," which at the time was a term used by psychiatrists to indicate someone with mild mental disabilities. She was shown to still be in the institution at the time of her death at the age of fifty-seven. Perhaps the story of her life is a mystery that is best left unsolved. The portraits illuminate two beautiful young girls, and they appear to be this age when their spirits show themselves. It is likely that this is the age when both girls were the happiest.

Also, on the second floor, at the top of the stairs, is a room containing many items belonging to John and Wilhelmina. The museum is fortunate to be in possession of some of Wilhelmina's beautiful gowns, including her wedding gown. This room has a warm, happy feeling, although it is unclear if this particular room was actually the couple's bedroom.

Never afraid to use the divining rods, Kathy has spoken to other ghosts who seem to be earthbound and tied to the objects from their lives. In the basement, there is a dentist's chair and implements that once belonged to Dr. Charles Keely. Dr. Keely was once a prominent dentist in Hamilton. He spent his entire life practicing a profession he loved until his eyesight started to fail him at the age of eighty-three. The fact that he could no longer

Left: Portrait of Anna Owens as a little girl, and as her spirit appears in the halls of the Butler County Historical Society. *Author's collection.*

Below: Portrait of Isabella Owens as a little girl and as her spirit appears playing in the hallway of the Butler County Historical Society. *Author's collection.*

continue his life's work made him despondent, and he took his own life. He went upstairs at his North Second Street home for a nap after lunch, which was his usual custom. It was then and there that he consumed a quick-acting potion. He left a note for his partner from the dentist office in the downtown Rentschler building that blamed his failing eyesight. Dr. Keely's home of many years on North Second Street was demolished to accommodate the building of the lovely Marcum Park. It appears that he has taken up residence just a half block away at the historical society, near his beloved tools of the trade that were used for years in the dental practice he lived for. Communicating through the divining rods, the doctor says he just doesn't understand why people are afraid of him or any dentist for that matter.

There are two Native American spirits who sometimes make their presence known to Kathy. One is Blue Jacket, and the other is Little Turtle. They were contemporaries who fought together in an American Indian alliance of Shawnee, Miami, Wyandot and a number of smaller tribes against U.S. military forces in the Ohio Country. This coalition of Indian tribes defeated General St. Clair, governor of the Northwest Territories, in the most severe defeat inflicted on the United States by Native Americans. Little Turtle led the first two battles, but it was Blue Jacket who fought the third and final

Left: Picture of Wilhelmina Benninghofen in younger years hanging in her bedroom. *Author's collection.*

Below: Wilhelmina Benninghofen's bedroom showcasing her wedding attire. *Courtesy of the Butler County Historical Society.*

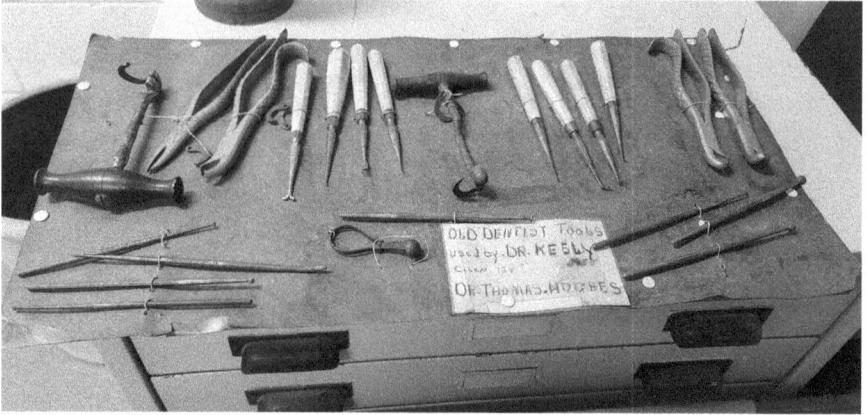

Dr. Charles Keeley's dental instruments can be found in the basement of the Butler County Historical Society near his dentist's chair. *Author's collection.*

battle. It was the crowning achievement of Blue Jacket's career, even though Little Turtle takes most of the credit.

The haunting of Blue Jacket involves a picture that hangs over the water fountain; it features Ollie Randall, who thought she was the great-great-great-niece of Blue Jacket. Although Blue Jacket was 100 percent Shawnee, he had two wives who were not. His first wife was a white woman, and his second wife was a quarter Native American. There was a legend that Blue Jacket was actually a white man, Marmaduke Van Swearingen, who was captured and adopted by the Shawnee in 1770 when he was a boy. The story goes he was wearing a blue wool jacket when he was taken. DNA tests have recently proven that Marmaduke was *not* Blue Jacket, and the ghost of the Indian is still trying to get the story straight for those who don't know. He is upset because people are still getting it wrong; he is the War Chief Blue Jacket, not Marmaduke Van Swearingen.

Little Turtle of the Miami tribes, who is the other war chief taking up residence at the museum, seems to be tied to his belongings on display there. After the peace treaty was signed following the Indian wars of the Northwest Territory, the Huston family settled outside of Oxford in an area now known as Huston Woods. They wanted something to show local Indians that they were given permission to be there, with the hope of warding off potential attacks. The nearby Native Americans were the Miami tribes, so the Hustons asked Little Turtle to give them some items to show the encroaching Indians. Little Turtle obliged by giving them one of his ceremonial tomahawks (which is currently in the museum

Painting of Marmaduke Van Swearingen as Blue Jacket before DNA determined that he was *not* the famous Shawnee war chief. *Author's collection.*

and has been verified as authentic by the Smithsonian Institution) and a handmade shovel. What makes it appear as though Little Turtle is tied to his possessions is what happened when these items were shipped to the statehouse in Columbus for a six-month exhibit on the Native American story. While the tomahawk was on loan to the state exhibit, Little Turtle was incommunicado. It is believed that he followed his belongings to Columbus, because when the items returned, Little Turtle was again communicating.

The instances of spirit communication at the Butler County Historical Society are frequent and many. To experience the hauntings firsthand, you should join one of the tours and determine the truth for yourself.

5

HAUNTED LAW OFFICE

On the western edge of German Village, adjacent to St. Julie Billiart's Catholic Church and very close to Marcum Park and the Great Miami River, there stands a stone building that was constructed in 1861. This Civil War–era building was originally a home, but for seventy years it served as Cahill Funeral Home. Coincidentally, the owner died here.

Currently, this historic stone structure houses the law offices of McKenzie & Snyder, and according to the staff, strange occurrences have convinced them that the building is haunted. At one time, the structure sat next to St. Raphael's Convent for the Franciscan Sisters of the Poor. The Hamilton convent was established in 1942; the mission of the sisters was to provide food, clothing and help to the indigent, poor and anyone who needed it without question. One of the nuns, Sister Nathanael, was in charge of the Kennedy Center, which housed Catholic Charities beginning in 1954, as well as Hamilton Recovery Inc., an agency designed to help people with mental and emotional problems.

When in 1919 Funeral Director Cahill moved his operations to what is now currently the law office, he stored the bodies in a separate building until there was time to prepare them for burial. A covered walkway was installed between the buildings. It was in this area, where the bodies were stored, that clearly defined orbs flew in all directions and were caught on a cellphone camera in complete darkness.

Employees of McKenzie & Snyder noticed what they described as "weird things" beginning to happen as the space that was once a convent was

Law office of McKenzie & Snyder on the southern border of German Village in Downtown Hamilton. *Author's collection.*

renovated. It was during this time that office phones would ring each other without human intervention. The heavy front door would open all by itself. The staff would hear unusual bumping sounds and unexplained footsteps. Sometimes there were shadows moving about for no apparent reason and the lights in the computer room would go out. These compounding, unexplained anomalies were enough for them to call in a professional team because they wanted to know what was going on.

TriOPS (Tri-State Ohio Paranormal Society) came to investigate the building and render their professional opinion. In fact, society members visited the offices three times in all. And every time they were able to connect with spirits and record the results.

They performed their tests in complete darkness. In the basement, a penlight was placed on a chair and used to simply verify that spirit was present. When asked to do so, the light came on. Then went out on its own. To prove that the irregularity was not with the light, another light that was brand new and still in the packaging was opened, assembled and put on the chair. The process was repeated and resulted with the light illuminating in response to the investigator's request. An unexplained orb flew toward the light and disappeared as it merged with the beam. The investigators made contact with the spirit of a boy named Timmy that moved a chair and caused the flashlight to flicker. When the investigation was over and the flashlight was picked up while packing up the equipment, the light was described as being so cold that it could have been sitting in a bucket of ice.

Who are the ghosts in this former funeral home and nunnery? Mediums working with the paranormal group said that as they communicated with spirits with their divining rods, the rods kept aiming in the same direction. They said they made contact with the spirit of a young girl. They concluded that the girl had been living with the nuns and she had been given up by her family. She had a mental disability, and the family just didn't know what to do with her. Until 1955, people with mental and emotional disabilities were institutionalized and didn't remain in the home.

In 1946, Congress passed the National Mental Health Act and in 1949 researched ways to treat mental health in the communities. With Sister Nathanael responsible for Hamilton Recovery and the assistance of persons with mental and emotional health concerns it seems possible that the spirit of this young girl has every reason to hang out here. According to the paranormal investigators, her ghost sits in a window most of the time, looking out into the courtyard.

Finally, the investigators said they made contact with a boy and his mother whom they believe died in a fire in the attic. The owner of TriOPS said that he truly believed that ghosts are likely in this building, but they could provide no actual proof. In the three times they have investigated the law offices, they have never been disappointed.

6

THE WILD WEST COMES TO HAMILTON

A popular stop on the Dayton Lane Ghost Walk is the ancestral home of Christian Benninghofen, a prominent industrialist and son of John and Wilhelmina Benninghofen, who also appear in this book. This elegant home is popular not only because of its stately beauty and status as an easily recognizable landmark in the National Register of Historic Places, but it also has many interesting spirits and ghost stories. This house was built for Christian in 1892, significant because when the third-floor tenants were interviewed for the ghost walk in 2003 they mentioned that a particular history book regularly flew from the top shelf of the built-in bookcase. When the book was removed from the shelf where it was tightly sandwiched between two others and the leather cover was turned back, it revealed the copyright date 1892—the year the house was completed. Why this book only and not another of the hundred books sitting in the bookcase? There was no easy answer.

Christian Benninghofen was partner to William Shuler of Shuler & Benninghofen Woolen Mills, which was founded by Christian's father, John, and William's father, Asa. The company remained a partnership between the two prominent families. Christian was an astute businessman and a civic-minded public servant. He served on city council for many terms and was a leader in the Democratic Party. He lived nearly eighty-two years and died in his home, as was the custom. After first being afflicted with sciatica rheumatism, he suffered a bout of pneumonia from which he never recovered.

Listed in the National Register of Historic Places, the Christian Benninghofen mansion is currently offered as a short-term rental and it's haunted. *Author's collection.*

Who are the ghosts in this house? While gathering information for the ghost walk, there were three sources for the material that became the script for the historic yet spiritual event. The occupants of this house provided firsthand accounts, the psychic medium Victor Paruta walked through and gave his impressions and the Lane Public Library provided corroborating facts in the follow-up. According to our psychic medium, there are a minimum of four ghosts still occupying the house. A house of this size would have had more than just the family, including servants, cooks and possibly other staff. Some of the spirits have made themselves known to owners and tenants; some spoke only to our medium, who felt that Mr. Benninghofen, who died in March 1937 after severe pneumonia, is still in the house with his wife, Anna, caring for him, as in life. Victor spoke about the ghost of an additional woman who is still present, and the 1910 census lists a nineteen-year-old female servant. It could be her. There is the spirit or imprint of an old man, possibly Christian, who is in ill health; he shakes and has trouble walking. At the end of his life, Christian suffered from pneumonia and sciatica rheumatism, and you will notice in the picture of Christian

Christian and Anna Benninghofen posing outside the Benninghofen mansion. *Author's collection.*

and Anna that Christian carries a cane. It very likely could be Christian. Victor had to sit down in the hallway when connecting with this man; he was experiencing the old gentleman's irregular heartbeat.

Victor felt there was a sick child in the house who survived but may have had some permanent health issues. Christian had two sons and two daughters, but the health of his children is an unknown. However, it was later determined that at least one in the house had Spanish flu, supported by the memory of a neighbor's mother who recalled quarantine signs posted around the Benninghofen house at the time of the influenza pandemic of 1918–19. The pandemic infected a third of the entire world population, leaving millions of people dead. Patients suffering from what was often called the Spanish flu—which is a name that just caught on even though it didn't originate in Spain—easily caught pneumonia and some quickly died. There were no casualties that we know of in Christian and Anna's house, but Christian did unfortunately die in his home from complications following his own case of pneumonia in 1937.

It was reiterated that there is a strong male energy connected to this house; a little old guy with health issues, he was very demanding of his nurses and is German in demeanor, possibly a military gent. This old man is a resident ghost. Psychics freely admit that no one is a 100 percent correct, but Christian just happens to be a first-generation German American who was probably a strong and demanding person. After all, he ran an extremely

Left: Portrait of Christian Benninghofen, co-owner of Shuler & Benninghofen Woolen Mills. *Author's collection.*

Right: Balcony at Christian and Anna's house. *Author's collection.*

successful company and was a civic leader on many fronts. But according to a living relative, he was never unkind to family or friends.

There is quite a different energy in the sitting room on the second floor. In his reading, Victor spoke of a man connected with a rodeo who would climb up the outside steps to the balcony to see the girl who slept in the bedroom there. As the parade would pass by on Dayton Street from the Butler County Fairgrounds, he would look toward her window, where she would sit on the elevated porch. Victor felt she was a teenager, and the cowboy would tip his hat to her as he passed by. The relationship was discouraged, however, because of the difference in social classes. This would have taken place in the late nineteenth or earlier twentieth centuries. Could this cowboy be affiliated with Buffalo Bill's Wild West Show, which paraded cowboys and Indians down Dayton Street to and from the fairgrounds? Or maybe it was Pawnee Bill's Wild West Show. Pawnee Bill sometimes appeared with Buffalo Bill until he formed a show of his own. Both shows paraded their livestock and stars through town; however, the street parades were discontinued in 1907. Victor also had a strong sense of the West in the back parlor, a feeling that they may have entertained the visitors while in town. Pawnee Bill was

Left: Buffalo Bill Cody, head of the Wild West Show. *J. Willis Sayre Collection of Theatrical Photographs.*

Right: Studio portrait of Pawnee Bill (Gordon W. Lillie) with a moustache, long hair and a cowboy hat. *Denver Public Library Special Collections.*.

known to have many friends in the city of Hamilton and in Butler County. The timing would be right. The 1910 census reports that there were four women living in the house: Christian's wife, Anna; his twenty-seven-year-old unmarried daughter, Elsa; his seventeen-year-old daughter, Margarite; and his nineteen-year-old servant, May Raum. However, there is no evidence that this occurred, and to quote Christian's great-great-granddaughter, "I talked to my mom about the cowboy stuff. She was born in 1917 so would have heard any such tales. None. No tales." History supports the possibility, but there are no facts to prove it was true.

"I never felt comfortable in the library, scared actually." This comment was made by an occupant who lived in the house for many years. The comment was posed to Victor as he toured the house for the purpose of the ghost walk. It was his belief that her unease in the library was because women were not welcome in a "man's business." A more believable proposition and a verified possibility for her discomfort is that a maid was electrocuted in the library. As related by a Christian Benninghofen descendant, "There was a maid electrocuted in the library. They have

Library in the home of Christian Benninghofen, where a maid was said to have electrocuted herself while vacuuming and still haunts the house. *Author's collection.*

electrical plugs on the floor, and I think she sprayed a cleaner on it. This was according to my mom, Eleanor Benninghofen, who grew up in the house for part of her life....We never told [J...] about the maid because we were worried she would freak out a little."

The former homeowner who was afraid to go into the library had the following to say about her experience in the house. She admitted that she often felt tugging on her hand during twilight sleep in her master bedroom. During his tour, Victor sensed her bedroom at one time was the room of a nurse who cared for an elderly woman. Her patient stayed in the turret bedroom on the second floor that adjoined the master bedroom. His suggestion was that the ghost of the nurse was tugging at this individual for help with her charge. Using his words, the second-floor bedroom has a positive female energy and a loving vibe. He could feel the death of someone in the house and the subsequent wake. This was a common practice until the middle of the twentieth century. This female energy took the death in stride; she was a good listener and a natural psychologist, comforting and encouraging. The unmarried daughter of Christian and

Anna died in the house of cancer at the age of forty-nine, and it is thought that this was her bedroom. The belief is that the nurse is still caring for her in the spirit world and making her presence known to the then current owner. The explanation from Christian's descendant: "We think that might have been Elsa Benninghofen's room. She died of pancreatic cancer." Elsa was the unmarried daughter of Christian and Anna who lived with them until she died suddenly at the age of forty-nine. Elsa had devoted herself to the study of piano, and her charming personality endeared her to her many friends and family.

There were multiple experiences related by this occupant of the Benninghofen house, other than the fear of the library and the bedroom experience. According to this person, "A young girl appears at the top of the main stairwell always sitting on the stained-glass windowsills. Long hair with a bit tied back with a white ribbon and in a blue dress." It is not known who this might be; there were two Benninghofen daughters, one of whom died in the house, and young servants who maintained this large mansion, including the one electrocuted in the library. It could have been any of them. The *Hamilton Evening Democrat* of June 27, 1901, may provide a clue: "Miss Gretchen Benninghofen entertained at a birthday party yesterday afternoon at her home on Dayton street. Miss Benninghofen received her guests on the lawn and wore a very pretty white swiss dress with blue ribbons." Could this be the spirit of the young lady in the window seat? Margaret Gretchen Benninghofen Werner died in 1984 at the age of ninety-one.

The young girl in the window seat is not the only spirit this person has seen. Her first ghostly encounter was a woman in a black dress with her hair neatly tucked into a bonnet. She showed up while the owner was tiling a bathroom in a second-floor apartment in what was originally Mr. Benninghofen's bedroom. The apparition was simply watching curiously; there was nothing to be afraid of. But the owner screamed, dropped her trowel and ran downstairs. After she experienced this fright, she ran into the curious ghost again, this time at the Butler County Historical Society. During her visit there she saw a photo of the woman in a bonnet that she saw while placing the bathroom tile. In the dining room of the Butler County Historical Society, on the wall, there was a picture of the woman who visited her in the second-floor apartment. She was a servant to the Benninghofen family. "I was absolutely blown away when I saw it! I still believe and feel that her name was Heather or Hannah. That bathroom I was in is just outside of what was Mr. Benninghofen's master bedroom at the back of the second floor."

There seem to be so many spiritual presences in the Benninghofen mansion that, in an attempt to find out who shared the space but couldn't be seen, an area paranormal investigation group, TriOPS Paranormal Research, was invited in to see what they could find. Their most significant finding was the report that they saw bodies being housed in the basement, but historical research didn't produce anything factual to verify that. The only possible link could be the practice that when people died in their homes, the body would be laid out and services held right there. It is a fact that family funerals were held in this home, and it is possible that the cool basement might have been used in some capacity to keep the bodies fresh until burial. The TriOPS investigators felt there were bodies in the basement because of the 1913 flood, but according to the Benninghofen family, there is no truth in that.

7

THE TRIAL OF THE CENTURY

A crowd of over one hundred spectators gathered outside what is now a three-story Second Empire mansion. This house underwent extensive renovations early in the twentieth century to add a third floor, changing the architectural style from Italianate, popular in the Dayton Lane Historic District during the nineteenth century, to a unique red-tiled mansard-roofed home. Residences of this design were generally large and built for the affluent homeowner, and at the turn of the century, this neighborhood was known for the rich families who lived here. The group edged in closer to hear the stories offered by the current homeowner. The night was cool and smelled of molting leaves recently fallen; the darkness simply added to the atmosphere of excitement. The visitors hoped for a chance to see proof of some of the stories they were hearing that night. The front door was open to the house, and the owner wore a black top hat and held a softly lit candle to create an ambiance that would enhance his narrative. While telling of the "Lady" on the stairs he turned in the doorway to point to the open stairway, and there she appeared! He quickly turned back to the crowd, scattering hot wax toward the front row. Some in the crowd were granted their wish and saw the vaporous image on the stairs.

Over the years, many prominent people have lived in this notable house on Dayton Street. It was built for Cora Hoagland, heiress to the Royal Baking Powder fortune, as a wedding present by her husband, George Tangemann. Was Cora the lady on the stairs? Not likely, for they soon moved to Oyster Bay, New York, where they could be close to the company operations.

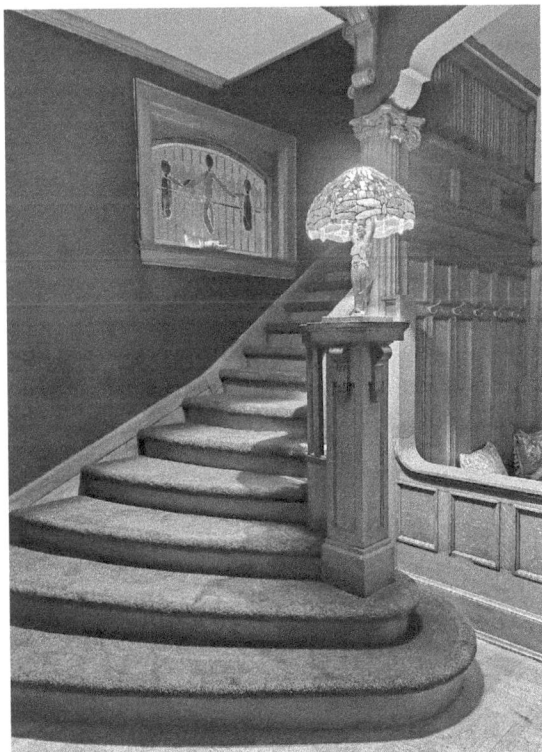

Above: Early in the twentieth century, Aaron Campbell's Italianate house was heavily remodeled to add a third floor and a French mansard roof. *Author's collection.*

Left: Campbell mansion stairway where "The Lady" was seen by a group of ghost walk attendees, among many others. *Author's collection.*

Home to A.L.S. Campbell and occasional residence of his father, William H.H. Campbell. It was taken from him in the Trial of the Century. *Lane Public Library Cummins digital collection.*

The house, at that time still a more modest Italianate structure, was sold to William H.H. Campbell, one of the wealthiest men in Butler County. William bought this house for his eldest son, Aaron L.S. Campbell. William bought houses for each of his children; two still stand in the Dayton Lane neighborhood, this one and the McKinney house two doors down on the corner. Although she rarely lived there, the house belonged to Fannie. Since the norm in those days didn't allow women to own property, the rents and equity went to her husband.

Aaron, a favorite of his father, increased the family fortune through the creation and operation of several icehouses that supplied Cincinnati and Hamilton's many malthouses and breweries. When William's health declined Aaron took care of his father and the family businesses.

Fannie married the manager of Fay Templeton, a famous burlesque star who excelled on the legitimate and vaudeville stage for more than half a century. Fannie's marriage was a turbulent one and caused her to end her life at the young age of thirty after only five years of marriage. Could Fannie be haunting the house of her brother, the house that her father used as his townhouse? Only a few months before Fannie killed herself, her father and brother Aaron committed her to an asylum in Oxford. She had to call on her cheating and abusive husband to file a writ of habeas corpus to get her released. Fannie committed suicide just days after divorcing her husband. William H.H. Campbell never did get over Fannie's death. After she overdosed on morphine, it is said that he regularly made a trip to the post office to send her money, forgetting that she was dead. William died just four short years after Fannie, never getting over her death and any part he may have played.

What followed the patriarch's death was a long-drawn-out legal battle that became known as the "Trial of the Century." It took place in the last decade of the nineteenth century at the Butler County Courthouse. Those who knew William H.H. in those years preceding his death couldn't determine if he was an incorrigible drunk or simply crazy. Aaron Campbell, loyal son, protégé and guardian in his father's declining years was rightful heir to the family fortune. Following this extended lawsuit—in which when Aaron lost the house gifted to him by the old gentleman and the Campbell fortune changed hands from Aaron to less deserving relatives—misfortune surrounded the family like a black cloud. Aaron died a penniless man, the sisters involved in successfully suing Aaron died early deaths and the nephew who was named executor after winning the lawsuit disappeared and to this day has never been found. The ghosts seen and heard in this house are more than likely the Campbell family

After Aaron lost his house to his nephew because of that trial, the home was sold to J.E. Wright, vice president of the Columbia Carriage Company, followed by Aaron and Clara Jacobs and their extended family. It was Aaron Jacobs who added the third floor to accommodate his large family. The third floor was added to the building, and it was extensively remodeled in the Second Empire style. The three families all lived in the house, which at that time was considered one of the most elegant in the city according to the *Hamilton Daily Republican News*. And since Victor sensed no apparitions whatsoever on the third floor, the ghosts in this house are more than likely from an earlier era.

Where did the story of the lady on the stairs begin? On a sunny late spring day during a Dayton Lane biennial fundraiser known as the May Promenade, an elderly lady stopped at the garden gate to have her ticket validated. She told the story of her time as one of the house staff at 622

Dayton Street decades earlier. She worked as a cook for the family living here at the time for many years. While in their employ, she saw, on multiple occasions, a young woman on the master stairway at the front of the house. The apparition's features were not visible since she was merely a gray wisp that floated to the bottom of the grand staircase before disappearing. Now one might say the "lady" was a figment of the old woman's imagination, but what would you say if the apparition appeared to more than just this person? During the same event, a group of Red Hatters came through the house. The ladies of this organization are recognizable because they all wear red hats. The hats indicate that they are members of an international group of women dedicated to reshaping the way women are viewed in today's culture. These ladies were once members of the Hamilton First Pilgrim Holiness Church, which was located in this building. Two of the three women were eyewitnesses to the young lady on the stairs following a worship service. These women were not familiar with the elderly cook who told a similar story.

There is also the ghost of a man in this house that stays in the back bedroom on the second floor. This man believed in Spiritualism and tried to connect with his mother after she passed. He was a private man, kept to himself and felt that people were an intrusion. He merely wanted to be alone with his imagination. His spirit is surrounded by a mix of soft music and Sousa marches. He was a very proud man and fastidious in his appearance. He loved his parents so much that when they passed, he was a changed man. They died when he was between the ages of thirty-six and forty-two years old. When they passed, he became despondent. These, anyway, are the impressions of our medium Victor. It fits that this spirit could be the spirit of Aaron Campbell, who regularly attended a Unitarian church, which could explain a leaning toward spiritualistic beliefs. If it is Aaron, he would have lived in this house when he was thirty-eight years of age to forty-four. Aaron lived to his mid-sixties, so his spirit in this house would reflect his age when he occupied the house in life, not when he died. He died a poor man living on a farm he rented after being one of the wealthiest men in the county. The aftereffects of the Trial of the Century after his father's death certainly could have caused him to be despondent.

Another resident ghost is a young lady who in some way is related to the man in the second-floor bedroom. Could it possibly be the mother that he longs for? If it is his mother, she appears as a young woman. This lithe little spirit grew up on a farm in life. William H.H. Campbell raised his family on his farm outside of Hamilton, part of which is now Greenwood Cemetery.

Possibly it could be another of Aaron's sisters, Lelia perhaps. Lelia was considered a black sheep in the Campbell family, always at odds with her brother Aaron and with her father, who would always take Aaron's side of an argument. Her father, William H.H., also bought a house for her, just like he did for all her brothers and sisters. But Lelia's was a small frame house in a Dayton neighborhood that was nothing like Millionaire's Row, where the rest of her siblings had houses. She was one of the plaintiffs in the trial against Aaron to deprive him of his inheritance, a trial that she and three other family members won. Poor Lelia also died young, around the age of forty, before getting her inheritance. According to the death certificate, she died from a complication of diseases. Maybe it's Lelia not allowing her brother peace, even in death.

Victor felt the young lady had a connection to a horse and buggy. Is she connected to J.E. Wright of Columbia Carriage Company? It certainly would seem a possibility. He lived here just a short while, but then so did the Campbells. However, the times were far less tumultuous during the period when the Wrights lived in the house. It could also indicate a connection to the Campbells, who lived here in the 1890s. After all, William H.H., who frequently stayed in the house with his son Aaron, was often found in a drunken stupor in his carriage while his horse wandered through town.

What has manifested that serves as evidence for the otherworldly souls who occupy this house? Occasionally, in the second-floor hallway midway down the hall near the back bedroom, there is a strong scent of flowers. This same overpowering smell of flowers has been sensed on the stairs as well as the hallway off the parlor on the first floor. In the same first-floor hallway a soft sobbing has been heard, but once you step over the threshold to the parlor, the crying subsides. This incident occurred during one of the ghost walks when one of the owners was outside the front door waiting for his turn to address the crowd, and his wife was in the office trying to be very quiet so she wouldn't distract the guests. She was aware of the hush of the gathering; the sobbing wasn't coming from them. It lasted only a couple minutes and stopped when she went to the parlor to wait on the sofa.

Many people have seen "The Lady" over the years, and only those incidents where individuals have come forward have been included in this book. While this home was the Children's Diagnostic Center, the woman would appear descending the stairway from the landing but would disappear before reaching the bottom. While the house was used as a church, some members of the congregation observed the same vision. On a home tour several years ago, certain guests noticed the same lady floating down the staircase during the tour.

While working on the renovation of the second-floor bathroom, a construction worker sensed a man looking over his shoulder approvingly. He was reluctant to say anything and didn't mention it for quite some time—not until the man of the house stopped to talk to him during demolition and happened to bring up his own experience. He had encountered a ghost who appeared in what is now a second-floor kitchen. He walked in to fetch a sandwich and a cold beer only to find an opaque figure of a man dressed in period clothing and standing next to the refrigerator. Once spotted, the figure disappeared.

Early in the morning while her husband was still in bed, the woman of the house was in that same bathroom getting ready for work. She was looking in the mirror when out of the corner of her eye she saw someone pass by the bathroom door in the dark hallway. She stepped into the hall, thinking it was her husband, and saw something turn into the back bedroom. Still thinking it was her husband, she searched through the dark to see if he was up and possibly in the kitchen or back bedroom, but upon investigation nothing was found. Many times, also on the second floor, she heard what she thought was her husband calling her name. Thinking he was home from work early in the day, she looked around trying to find him. No one was in the house or on the outside grounds. They insist that none of these encounters is their imagination.

The homeowner, during a period when his wife was working out of the country, decided to surprise her by wiring the newel post for a light. In order to do that, he had to break through a concrete brick wall off the landing in the basement stairwell. There are several rooms in the basement full of silt from the 1913 flood that were walled off, and this was one of them. He stood on the landing wearing a headlamp since it was pitch dark in the sealed-off room. Before crawling through the small opening, he felt the landing move beneath his feet. He had a strange feeling in the pit of his stomach, but that didn't deter him. He slid through the opening and shimmied across the room full of silt on his stomach until he found the correct location for running the wire to the post. While in the room of silt, in the process of completing his project, he found an old pair of cobbled shoes. He feared what else might be beneath the eight feet of river silt. How did the old weather-worn shoes get there, and who did they belong to? Only a couple of people over the years have ventured to the cellar; they find it uncomfortable.

8

"BROTHER CAN YOU SPARE A DIME"

THE GREAT DEPRESSION IN HAMILTON

Opposite Campbell Avenue Park is a lovely brick Georgian Revival house. It was built in 1909 for August Fischer, the vice president of the Ohio Tile Company. This beautiful home is called the Reister House after August's nephew Jacob Reister, who lived in the home from 1930 to 1944. But if you are a local to the neighborhood, you know it as the Cat Lady's House. Why such a strange moniker, you may ask.

Victor Paruta climbed the stairs and then slowly and thoughtfully walked through the hallway leading to French doors that open to the second-story porch. As he moved through the space, heading toward the doors, he felt something flying about his head. In his words, it felt like the hall was full of paper airplanes whizzing by. That was a strange reading. No one could relate to his comments at the time, but later the reason for his unusual observation was discovered as longtime residents in the neighborhood who worked with Sherry Corbett came forward.

We know that prior to restoring this building, there were many holes in the windows and roof. Sherry Corbett, now deceased, restored many of the homes on Campbell Avenue, the Reister House being one of them. During restoration, she found pigeon excrement everywhere on the upper floors of the house. The story goes that a previous owner, dubbed by Sherry as the Cat Lady, allowed them to fly freely throughout the house. The impressions of those birds are still evident in the house to those who are sensitive to it.

In the midst of the flying spirit birds on the second floor, Victor tuned into two men who met on the balcony studying maps or blueprints that

Jacob Reister House, home to August Fischer and much later to the woman Sherry Corbett named the "Bird Lady." *Author's collection.*

they spread out on a table. He placed these men around the time of Teddy Roosevelt (1901–9). That would indicate they are from the time when August Fischer first built the house, and maybe the blueprints they are studying are of the house that he's building. Victor felt the other man was one who visited often. This frequent visitor was involved in developing land or financing mortgages. He felt that the owner during that time, which certainly would have been August Fischer if his timeline is correct, had a hand in building or architecture. As Fischer was vice president of the Ohio Tile Company, it's reasonable to assume that it could have been him.

August transferred the deed to his house to his nephew Jacob Reister in 1928. There are numerous other ghosts present in this house from different periods, but Victor mostly sensed that these ghosts were from the 1930s through the '40s. Some of his impressions have been validated, yet others are still a mystery. The large three-story house was home to Jacob Reister's extended family during the Great Depression, with many people living there from 1930 to 1944. At that time, residents would have included Jacob's wife, Sarah; his adult son Fred, who was an attorney; his adult daughter Evelyn, who was employed as a secretary for the railroad; his mother-in-law, Anna Hayes; and his widowed uncle, August Fischer, whose wife, Sadie, died in 1924. It was a large family for sure, but also a large house.

Jacob Reister was a freight agent for the CH&D (Cincinnati-Hamilton & Dayton) Railroad. Like his uncle, Jacob was well liked. According to the 1916 *Republican* newspaper, he was one of the most important reasons for the popularity of the railroad freight service among the shippers of Hamilton and the surrounding area. Jacob was one of its most valued employees. He retired from the railroad on January 1, 1940, due to ill health and died suddenly of a heart attack in his home only a month later. His wife, Sarah, died just two years later at the age of sixty-four. The home stayed in the Reister family until 1950.

Many ghosts and impressions were found in the Reister House. Immediately as he approached the home and walked up the steps to the large tiled front porch, Victor sensed two ghosts, a male and a female who both lived to be very old. August lived to be seventy-seven, and Anna Hayes, Jacob's mother-in-law, lived to ninety-eight.

The third floor is an open loft-type apartment with warm wood paneling all around. Victor tuned into what he felt was an imprint rather than an actual ghost. There, looking out the window was an old lady who was frail and unstable. He sensed she was emotional as she looked out the window at a parade, a parade of soldiers honoring someone important who died, like a president or general. This woman, dressed in a bonnet and old-fashioned clothes, was watching what could have been a funeral procession from the third-story window. It's possible this could allude to Brigadier General Ferdinand VanDerVeer of the Civil War, who was buried in Greenwood Cemetery. His procession would certainly pass through the neighborhood. And Greenwood Cemetery is only blocks away.

Also on the third floor, there was a sense of a secret passageway, but the area was searched, and nothing could be found that opened to a passage. There happen to be several curious doors that merely lead to open attic space. The owners weren't aware of any hidden passages in the house.

When entering the kitchen in the second-floor apartment, Victor found something that would be significant to what later appeared in the backyard. He spoke of a kind-hearted woman who invited those less fortunate to dine at her table during the 1930s and '40s. She enjoyed baking pies and feeding people and loved children. She suffered ill health though. If, in fact, this is Sarah Reister, she passed away in 1942 in the waning years of the Great Depression. She was known in life to be a kind and giving person.

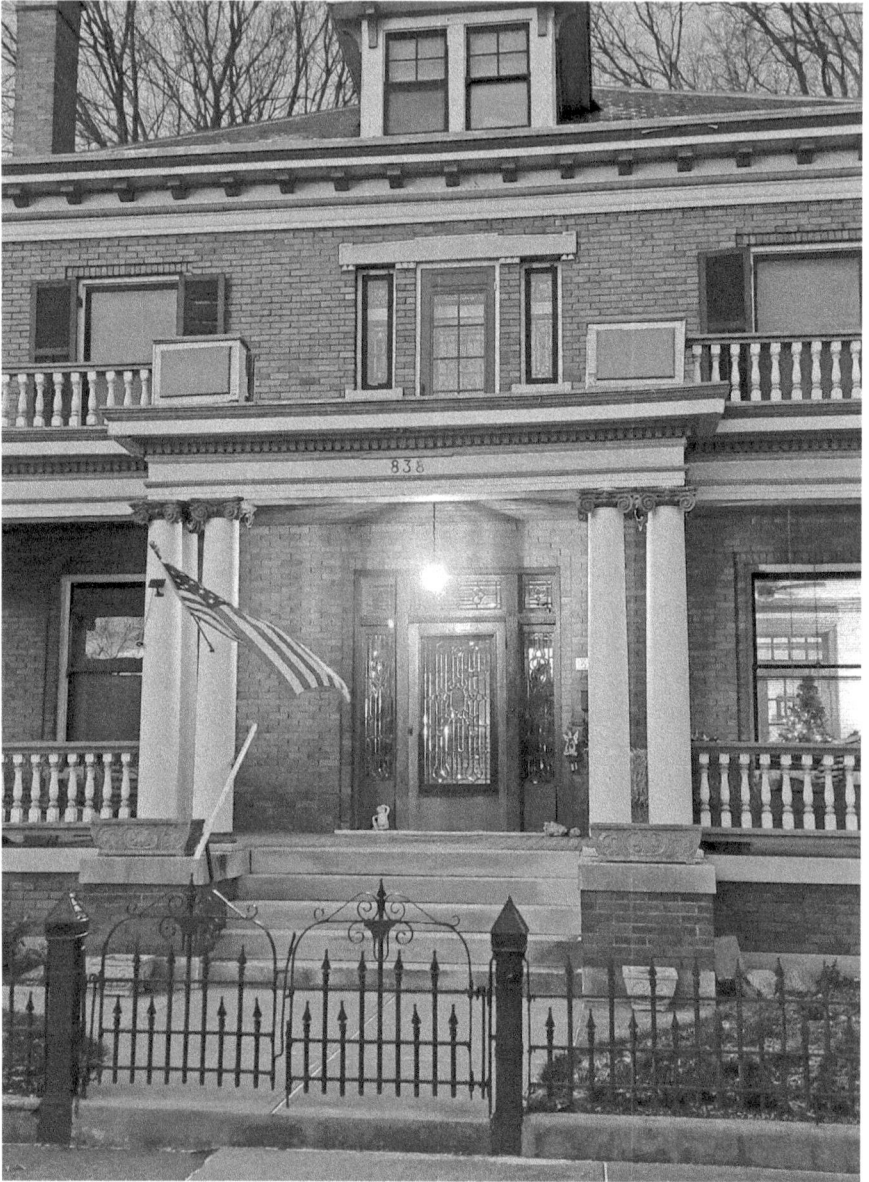

The Jacob Reister House at dusk. *Author's collection.*

During the Great Depression, laborers, poor and ragged, would sit around hoping for odd jobs and food, upset about their predicament. *Public domain.*

It was dusk as the group walked out of the house. They were drawn to the backyard, and once they stepped through an arbor that was positioned in the center of the yard they were suddenly overcome with a forlorn feeling, an unexplained anxiety. Victor commented that in the back half of the yard, between the arbor and the alley, there was a crowd of souls who in life used to wait patiently for some reason. He felt they were laborers, poor and ragged. He also felt a sense of resentment against the wealthy people who lived in the Dayton Lane district and that the outcasts were sitting around hoping for odd jobs and food. They were upset about their predicament. Since the ghosts gathered so near the alley, it would make sense that they could jump off the train just two blocks down before it reached the Fifth Street station.

During the Great Depression, Hamilton was known for its industry; it was very much a manufacturing town. Across the country, millions of American workers lost their jobs. In Ohio, by 1933 more than 40 percent of factory workers were unemployed. People had a difficult time supporting their families and took work wherever they could find it.

The Sanborn Fire Map illustrates railroad tracks running through the East End of Campbell Avenue Park. *Lane Public Library–Hamilton Sanborn Insurance Maps digital collection.*

According to the Sanborn Fire Maps, the railroad tracks ran along Erie Highway and passed through Campbell Avenue Park, just two blocks east of the Reister home. Many unemployed who were forced to search for jobs to support their families heard about work as far as hundreds of miles away...or even half a continent away. Often the only way they could get there was by hopping on freight trains, illegally. More than two million

74

THE BREAD LINE. HIGH SCHOOL BLDG. HAMILTON, OHIO. FLOOD.

Like the 1913 flood, the Depression brought long food lines for people who didn't know where to find their next meal. *Lane Public Library Cummins digital collection.*

men and perhaps eight thousand women became hoboes, forced to ride the rails in their search for work. Is that how the crowd found their way to the backyard of the Reister house?

Families, including those in Hamilton, were financially unable to scrape up money for their next meal. Bread lines and soup kitchens were established by charitable organizations, giving away bread and soup to the impoverished. These poor souls were constantly thinking about food and how they would find their next meal. Figuring out what they could eat was a daily task. The kindness thought to be offered by the Reister household could surely be an explanation for the gathering of ghosts in the backyard.

The hungry and unemployed developed a series of symbols in order to "talk" to one another. They left messages so that others would get the information about which homes were friendly and where they could find work or food. It sounds as though one of those homes was Cat Lady's House, that is, the Reister home.

9

DOWNTOWN HAUNTS

Hamilton is the Butler County seat and boasts a beautiful historic courthouse placed in proximity to the High-Main bridge in downtown Hamilton at the west end of the downtown corridor. The name of this main thoroughfare on the east side of the bridge is High Street, and it boasts beautiful historic buildings. This is the third iteration of the courthouse; the first was completed in 1803, the second in 1817 and the cornerstone for the building that stands today says 1885. A fire on March 14, 1912, began in the clock tower because of faulty wiring. Many were injured, and two died in that fire. A fireman and one other man were fatally crushed when the high tower came crashing down on top of them, burying them in the burning debris. The original clock tower was replaced by a smaller tower; otherwise, the building is the same as the 1885 Second Empire stately building. If walls could talk, the courthouse walls must have many stories to tell, as it has witnessed the history of many of Hamilton's citizenry. Certainly, it has its share of ghostly visitors. It is said that one of those ghosts is the spirit of a man who was hanged in the previous courthouse, before the current structure was built. In the 1860s, he was accused of stealing from the county. Some said he took his own life. Others say he was murdered, and he materializes to hunt down the men who framed him for the theft before murdering him. Is he still walking the halls of this historic beauty? Or is he just the result of overactive imaginations?

In 1913, Hamilton experienced the worst flood on record. There were floods in 1898 and 1907, but they didn't compare to the devastation brought to the city by the rapid rise of the Great Miami River in March 1913. The river rose approximately thirty feet in forty-eight hours. Three public-use bridges and the railroad bridge collapsed. By nightfall on March 25, the river was rising three feet per hour. Over 75 percent of the city was overcome by floodwaters, and many were stranded on rooftops and treetops, waiting to be rescued. Over one hundred people died in this catastrophic event, and many of the dead were stored in the basement of the Butler County Courthouse. Are those souls wandering the halls still? Maybe that's the reason for the eerie sensation as you walk the marble halls of this historic institution.

Down the street from the courthouse on South Second Street used to be the location of the Jefferson Theater built in 1903, renamed the Smith Theater in 1908. You won't find it standing there today; it was engulfed in flames in 1928 and burned to the ground. But long before the destruction and shortly after it was built in 1903, it attracted a large crowd to witness Dr. Amos H. Wayne bringing forth spirits of the dead. He held his séance in the light of day, to cast no doubt on the authenticity of his spiritualistic talents. A world-famous medium, he had been startling audiences with his famous séances not in darkness but in open light. The London spiritualist said that the forms seen and recognized by the audiences were conclusive proof that they are genuine spiritual manifestations. Eminent scientists were invited to test him to determine his authenticity. He attempted to demonstrate spirit power by the production of spirit pictures, materialization of forms and faces, clairvoyant tests, floating tables and chairs, invisible hands carrying flowers to guests in the audience and all this in open light. In 1903, Spiritualism would have been prevalent in the English-speaking world, as indicated by the popularity of Dr. Wayne in America, Britain, Germany and France. Even small-town Hamilton had a spiritualist church on High Street, where the Butler County Administrative Center stands today.

Farther east on the south side of High Street is another magnificent building with a rose window. This lovely example of Romanesque and Renaissance Revival architecture began as the Dixon Opera House in 1866, the year displayed on the raised brick parapet above the building. In 1889, Dixon sold the theater to William Frechtling, who renamed it the Globe Opera House. Frechtling, a retailer, turned the premises into the Robinson-Schwinn department store in 1907. Today, after an elaborate restoration project, it is home to Miami University Hamilton Downtown Campus and a number of professional offices.

Adjacent and attached to the old opera house is a restaurant, which at this writing is Basil 1791. The structure that now houses Basil 1791 and used to

Robinson-Schwinn building, home to Miami University's downtown campus, was originally the Dixon Opera House and then the Globe Theater. *Isaac and Alex Singleton, via Wikimedia Commons*.

be Ryan's Tavern has numerous firsthand accounts of poltergeist activity and hauntings. The Basil 1791 restaurant staff have felt touches to the shoulder, heard disembodied whispers and have seen water and lights turn on and off. The infamous ghost, Elizabeth, has been helping in the kitchen.

In 2008, Ryan's Tavern was opened by Don Ryan, once Hamilton's mayor, and the Irish pub in downtown Hamilton remained open until 2017. The front part of the structure was built in 1880, with the adjoining building behind it completed in 1890. It withstood the disastrous 1913 flood in Hamilton and has housed many kinds of businesses. While it was Ryan's Tavern, it boasted bars on the first and second floors and a private party

Ryan's Tavern, now Basil 1791 and home to several active ghosts. *Google Earth image capture.*

room also on the second floor. And when you entered Ryan's, you would find a warm, gregarious man named Tully greeting patrons as they walked through the double doors. Tully was the general manager of Ryan's for more than a decade, and does he have stories to tell about the 140-year-old downtown establishment, real encounters that made him a believer. Tully is no stranger to working in old historic buildings, but in his words, none was so haunted as this one. "I've worked in several old buildings in the area, historic buildings, and this one is definitely one of the most haunted I've ever been in. Some of the stories are amazing, and some of the things I've personally witnessed make me a believer."

The kitchen supervisor, someone who was a skeptic because of her spiritual beliefs, had a change of heart because of things that happened in her presence that just could not be explained. When asked if she now believes in the paranormal, she responded, "I do now because of experiences. Before I was kind of up in the air because of my spiritual beliefs. But my experiences, um, you can't explain." Strange things happened while she was in the ladies' restroom. She was the only person in the room, and while she was in one of the stalls of the two-stall restroom she heard noises in the stall next to her, then scratches on the wall. The scratching continued, and suddenly the door to the restroom slammed shut loudly. The door is large and difficult to close because it was misaligned; it would hit the wall instead of fitting into the door jamb. But the door closed on its own, fitting perfectly in the frame.

In the 1921 room, the formal dining room on the second floor, during one of the TriOPS investigations, photos were taken with a motion-detection camera that showed the form of a child peeking from behind a chair and a woman by the name of Antoinette sitting in the back of the room. The child could be Patricia, the spirit of a ten-year-old girl who plays in the basement.

TriOPS Paranormal Research has performed multiple investigations in Ryan's. They posted visible evidence of asking a question to the spirits and flashlights independently turning on and off in answer to the question. No one was even close to the flashlights. Shelving units have moved on their own. The third floor of the building is used for storage and is especially active. The tunnels in the basement, which were used for the smuggling of illegal alcohol during Prohibition, have been boarded up. The tunnels used to run the length of High Street to the river. Aside from the souls who seemed to be trapped there, you can say that the basement appears to be just a spooky place in its own right.

It has been said that the basement of the opera house also is haunted; it is currently used for storage. Spirits could be attached to the building for some reason, or they could be attached to the antiques that are stored down there. Who are the spirits that occupy the basement? No explanation has been offered. But when TriOPS placed their instruments on the sixteen-inch wall shared by the restaurant and the opera house, the device "lit up" with electromagnetic energy. What is going on?

Once a popular gathering place for Hamiltonians looking for amusement, the Dixon Opera House, which was renamed the Globe Theater, welcomed singers and dancers, comedians, acrobats, noted speakers and all forms of entertainment. At the dawn of the twentieth century, the remarkable Annie Oakley displayed her sharpshooting skills at the theater. In September 1901, a somber memorial service for President McKinley drew large crowds to honor the fallen president from Ohio who was assassinated by an anarchist in Buffalo, New York.

In 1911, a writer recalling the Globe Theater said, "For several years Hamilton enjoyed a distinction of being one of the best show towns in the Middle West," and the downtown opera house was a favorite stop for touring entertainers and theatrical companies. Over the years, it has been used for many purposes, so the spiritual activity could come from a variety of sources. It's evident that more research will be required to get answers.

10

PROHIBITION IN EAST HAMILTON

The Roaring Twenties and the Volstead Act, prohibiting the sale and consumption of alcohol, didn't pass by Hamilton, Ohio. Because the booze flowed freely, it attracted a criminal element, bringing prostitution and gambling along with it. The migration of the seedy side of life helped to earn Hamilton the nickname of "Little Chicago," mostly because of the connections that some of the citizens here had with the Chicago mob. One such family could be found on Dayton Street in the historic district.

The brown Prairie-style house at the corner of Eighth and Dayton Streets was owned by Raymond Walsh until his death. It is a lovely example of the type of architecture popularized by Frank Lloyd Wright. The house was built around 1920 by Charles Griesmer, a partner in Griesmer-Grim Undertakers, although it was his residence and never used as a funeral parlor. It has a warmth about it and appears to be a happy home with kindred spirits. And several ghosts have made their presence known to the current owners who call this house their home. One spirit is an older woman, slender and well dressed, who was a kind person in life. She stands next to the French doors that lead out to the large porch. She has blond hair and wears an "expensive" outfit the same color as her hair. Standing next to her is a man who is also outgoing, but he appears to dominate her. Laughter can be heard drifting down from the upstairs; the feeling is reminiscent of the glamor of old Hollywood from the 1930s.

Once the home of Raymond Walsh, who was involved with his brothers in illegal gambling operations. *Author's collection.*

Behind a door in the kitchen are stairs that lead you down to a full basement. It is in the basement where you can get the sensation of slot machines and the feeling that whoever lived in this house was somehow associated with illegal gambling. An elegant lady is present; she is standing near a man with thinning hair that he combs straight back. He is taking bets. Also in the basement is a fashionable guy, one who thinks he is quite the ladies' man. This spirit is connected to the blond female. They loved each other in life and love each other still. The lithe, beautiful woman was a younger version of the lady upstairs, and the man adored her. These are the sensations provided by Victor before the history of the house was researched to verify his account.

The people who live in the house now have sensed the essence of "people" being in the home with them, especially in the basement and on the third floor. They have seen individuals who seem to scurry away when confronted. The homeowners' two-year old son talked to his deceased grandfather, who came to visit him in his bedroom. Having never seen him, the little boy was miraculously able to describe him in vivid detail. Some say that children are more able to see spirits because they still have one foot in both worlds. According to many spiritualists, they are purer than most adults, more primeval, with no acquired filters. They haven't been told yet what to think or see. But ask a psychologist, and they will tell you that they have a harder time discerning what is real and what isn't. Children learn through imagination and pretend-play. So, they can slip easily between reality and fantasy. This is according to Dr. Aleta G. Angelosante, a child and adolescent psychiatrist at NYU Langone. Is grandfather a ghost? If you believe he is, then the spirit of the grandfather is the type that is attached to a person, as opposed to those that are bound to the house. This house has good examples of both. Yes, there are definitely ghosts in this house if one is open to the world of spirit.

There is an urban legend in the Dayton Lane Historic District that a numbers game was run from this house and that a prostitution and gambling ring was busted in the 1940s, thought to have been run from this house. Based on the history of the Walsh brothers, this may not be so much of an urban legend after all.

The Walsh brothers grew up in a small frame house in the 800 block of Dayton Street. Thomas, the oldest of the three brothers, was a bookie and co-owner of White's Cigar Store. White's Cigar Store was a front for betting on the horses and numbers racketeering. The patrons in the know would make their way to the back to feed the slot machines if that was their preferred method of gambling. Earlier, before the Walsh Café, Tom had an establishment in White City. According to the *Hamilton Daily News* of July 23, 1925, White City Park was known for all-night drinking, gambling and partying with underage girls, and the park was eventually closed down because of its illegal operations.

Tom met with a tragic and fiery end at only forty-one years of age when his roadster collided head-on with a train in Lindenwald, and he was burned beyond recognition. His car was wedged beneath the undercarriage of the train and fully engulfed in flames before anyone could get to him. At the time of his death, Tom was a proprietor of the Walsh Café at Fifth and Sycamore Streets, which passed to his brother John after his death.

The Walsh Café was a popular speakeasy during Prohibition, and John Walsh, the middle son, was a bootlegger and later proprietor of the café at Fifth and Sycamore Streets. In 1930, a moonshine still was seized south of Hamilton in violation of the Volstead Act, and John was fined $500, while two of his co-conspirators served time in the county jail for their misdeeds. As was common during Prohibition, his establishment was disguised as a "soda shoppe" where alcohol was served, a practice more common than one would expect. Besides alcohol, guests were offered gambling and slot machines while the police looked the other way. After many run-ins with the

Prohibition didn't stop the production and sale of alcohol, it just sent it underground. Hamilton had its share of speakeasies. *Getty Images, free image.*

law over selling alcohol, the cigar store/soda shop was shut down in 1933 and padlocked by the sheriff. But that didn't stop the Walsh brothers from carrying on with their illicit operations. In 1936, they built a new café at Fifth and Sycamore Streets. How fortunate for the Walsh Café that John's brother Raymond was in the business of supplying slot machines. When finally apprehended in 1949 for providing afterhours liquor sales and for offering gambling and slot machines for his patrons, John couldn't understand why it was suddenly a problem after at least seventeen years. John Walsh was indicted and went before the judge many times. Many who were arrested with him served jail time, but not John. He somehow managed to get by with no more than a fine.

The youngest son, Raymond, made his living providing slot machines for illegal gambling, including his brothers' café and cigar store. When Tom met his untimely death, Raymond was named executor of his will and inherited his brother's gambling enterprises. Raymond lived his entire life on Dayton Street, at first with his family at 830 Dayton before moving just three doors down from the family home to live out his life with his beloved wife, Aloise.

Raymond died of a massive heart attack in his home on Dayton Street in 1966. It is thought that he fell face-down into a plate of spaghetti before being transferred to Mercy Hospital, where he later died. Aloise continued to live in their home on Dayton Street until her death in 1985.

After hearing the story of the Walsh brothers, it makes so much sense that the gambling spirits can still be found in the basement of the Walsh home. The visions of those that still occupy this happy home on Dayton Street seem to align with the history of the close-knit family who lived here for much of the twentieth century. The current residents are willing to share their space and find the anomalies intriguing.

11

SPIRITS IN THE PARK

If you take a stroll down the cinder path running through Campbell Avenue Park at dusk, as the Victorian lamps that line the path blink on, your imagination will take you to another time. The autos in your peripheral vision disappear, and you are cloaked in the feeling of people and events from the past that surround you.

At the far end of the park is a wooded area that in the nineteenth century would have separated the neighborhood from the Erie Canal. In that dark wooded area, Victor, our medium, encountered ghostlike impressions of a boy in knickers and men fighting over cockfights or some kind of gambling. A man lying on the ground was carried away.

Somewhere in the park is the spirit of an unlucky soul, a man with the appearance of one with Down's Syndrome who is forever reliving his unfortunate death. His body was dumped near the 800 block of Campbell Avenue Park. An old man, possibly one of the gamblers from the wooded area, came to check on him, to see if he was alive. This old man was heavy, had gray hair and dressed in a duster-style overcoat. He found that the corpse had been badly beaten and then callously dumped in the park. The old guy can be seen trying to carry the body away. These types of images are difficult to validate, but since they were seen by an already proven psychic medium the imprint may have some element of truth to it. The demographic of Campbell Avenue was, and is, a mix of affluent owners and low-income tenants. An event such as this is conceivable in this area.

Campbell Avenue Park at twilight in the Dayton Lane Historic District. *Author's collection.*

At the southeast corner of Eighth and Campbell Streets, directly across from the Wolf Gazebo in the park, there is a beautiful "painted lady" Victorian home. In the 1890s, it was occupied by Daniel Hensley, Civil War soldier, teacher and postmaster of Hamilton appointed by President William Henry Harrison until he was removed by President Cleveland. It is a valid explanation of why Victor Paruta found a ghostly imprint of a mail delivery wagon as he walked through the park at this corner. The vision was of the horse slowing and someone jumping up to the worn wooden seat of the coach before the startled horse took off.

Continuing down the cinder path, past large stone urns with cascading flowers, past rounded stone benches for neighbors to sit and rest, Victor and those who followed him walked the Campbell Avenue neighborhood. He was attracted to Campbell Avenue Park by the feeling that he was walking among soldiers, visualizing them getting off a nearby train and carrying dead bodies on stretchers. If you have ever been to Dayton Lane, you know that there is no place to escape the shrill whistles of the trains that glide along the tracks in every direction. The entire historic district is surrounded by railroad tracks, then and now. There used to be tracks along the Erie Canal, which were removed when the canal was covered over. Today there are railroad tracks to the west of the district and to the south. A train station stands abandoned in a salvage yard two blocks south of the park and another abandoned station appears just a short distance along the west side of the district. His vision could very possibly be an imprint of things that occurred long ago. Trains transporting members of the armed services were familiar in Hamilton starting with the Civil War, which began in 1861.

The Civil War played an important role in this east-end neighborhood. Like many neighborhoods in Hamilton at the time, war-weary and wounded soldiers returned home to family and a different kind of life.

Because of the railroad and the access to water, this neighborhood especially was surrounded by Civil War encampments. Camp Hamilton initially was located at the Butler County Fairgrounds, just at the eastern edge of the district. Camp Hamilton was a training ground for Union soldiers, but there was not an adequate water source close by. It was relocated after a

War-weary Civil War soldiers, waiting to return home. *Photo via https://www.goodfreephotos.com.*

Once a campaign stop for President Abraham Lincoln during his 1859 run for office, the Hamilton station is dilapidated, abandoned and off-limits to the living. *Author's collection.*

short time to an area between the Miami Erie Canal and the Great Miami River on the west end of the district. Other than being the training ground for Union soldiers being sent off to war, Camp Hamilton later became one of the few horse veterinary encampments for warhorses. Significantly, the fact that the Dayton Lane Historic District and Campbell Avenue Park is in close proximity to the railroad and only a short distance to the train station where soldiers and livestock would come and go supports the visions that Victor had in the park of horses and soldiers.

Historical research shows that there were troops during the war camping on property owned by Lewis Campbell and delivering bodies to Greenwood Cemetery on the north side of the district. The research indicated that the camp was bordered by water on all sides. With the basin, hydraulic canal, Erie Canal and reservoir, the park could be the spot the account describes. Lewis D. Campbell, an advisor to Presidents Lincoln and Andrew Johnson, donated the stretch of land previously used as a racecourse to the city for use as a park, Campbell Avenue Park.

Many images came to mind as Victor passed through the park. One that stood out to residents was not a pleasant one. He walked slowly down the block and then came to a stop. He said he felt something evil, then pointed to a house across from the park. He had a malevolent feeling having to do with that house and wanted to move quickly past it, having no desire to find out anything more. The house was where the person who murdered Dr. Sherry Corbett, the district's matriarch, lived. Of course, the neighbors following him knew that, but Victor was never told how right he was.

12

THE McKINNEY MANSION AND CARRIAGE HOUSE

I n the late 1800s, an elegant and stately home was built at the gateway to the Dayton Lane Historic District for Robert C. McKinney, a prominent businessman who during his life in Hamilton was treasurer and general manager for Niles Tool Works, vice president of Beckett Paper Company and a vice president for the First National Bank. It was Robert who suggested the city turn the entire Campbell Avenue island into a park for the people. Robert and his wife often entertained in their beautiful home. It is a stylish half-timbered Queen Anne structure with three stories, seven ornate Victorian fireplaces, leaded and stained-glass windows. It includes an elaborate tri-part Oriel window that spans the north-side wall on the landing between the first and second floors. The first floor and stairway are adorned with pastoral murals, and the house was obviously built with an eye toward entertaining. Around the year 1890, the house was purchased by William H.H. Campbell for his socialite daughter Fannie, who rarely stayed in the house. Fannie committed suicide, and the house ultimately was sold to Thomas Curley.

Thomas Curley was the president of Columbia Carriage Company. He lived in the house with his sister and a servant until he went bankrupt and lost the house in a sheriff's sale in 1915. The house was converted to apartments in 1916, and in the years since, many people have passed through this house. Unfortunately, Columbia Carriage Company went into receivership in 1910–11 with the advent of automobiles and was bought out by three local businessmen who converted it into an automobile

The McKinney House at the Gateway of the Dayton Lane Historic District. *Author's collection.*

manufacturing company. While Curley lived in the main house, he made carriages on the second floor of the carriage house. On completion, the carriage would be wheeled down a ramp to the courtyard below. The first floor was used for horse stalls and those stalls are incorporated into the design of the apartments that are there today. The house remained in the possession of Ben Strauss, one of the businessmen who bought the carriage company for $42,000, until he sold it to Dr. Walter Pater in 1925.

When Victor visited this house, he found several ghosts. He said there was a lady of great social importance who held large balls and galas. She was the talk of the town. This was such a prestigious address and home to some very important people; this ghost could relate to several different people. However, Robert C. McKinney, who built the house, was a very wealthy businessman with a wife who entertained frequently in her home. He was the head of the Republican Party for Ohio and friends with the governor and president during his tenure here. It seems likely that it could refer to Mrs. McKinney. Some of the tenants have heard lots of party-type noises and music on the bottom floor of the house, even when they are alone.

Victor sensed someone often handing out food and other supplies to people that lined up at the back door of the house. He thought there were people "camped" in the courtyard at times. A possibility for this impression could relate to the fact that the Franciscan Sisters of the Poor lived here in the 1960s. Helping the poor and indigent was their mission in life. Maybe he was tuning into their vibrations. He got the sense that whoever it was could have been from an area church because he could "see" a church through the windows. The nuns also had a house next to St. Stephens Church farther down Dayton Street. The bell tower can certainly be seen from the third-floor windows. You definitely would hear the bells ringing for the call to prayer and the reciting of the Angelus at noon and 6:00 p.m. Even today, on Sundays you can hear the bells in Dayton Lane as they ring for the devotion.

Victor saw Sherry Corbett in this house, especially around Bob Sherwin's large first-floor apartment. Although he felt her presence in other areas too. Sherry and Bob worked together to restore the beauty of this house. Bob moved into the first-floor suite after Sherry's death, and he continued to run Corbett-Sherwin Victorian Rentals from a small apartment in the back, maintaining the house and carriage house until his death in 2018.

This large house has an equally large cellar with many rooms. The rooms are used for storage of food and antiques and includes a workshop, which comes in handy for the upkeep of the rental properties. In the basement are three ghosts, all three men. There was not a good vibe in the basement, only an uneasy feeling that the ghost at the bottom of the stairs was a pedophile or a similarly bad person. A second male spirit said "get out" and gave the impression that Victor was intruding in his home. This occurred in the carpenter's workshop at the far end of the basement. Finally, the third male spirit didn't give the impression that he was bad, just shy and didn't want to be bothered.

The investigative tour ended, everyone left. The caretaker was sitting in the office at the back of the house where the stairs lead to the basement, working at the computer. It's a small office with two steps that lead up to a tiny bedroom and an equally tiny kitchen. He thought he heard something and turned around to see a head, no body, just a head and shoulders peeking around the corner. He was alone in this part of the house; the group that had been going through the house had left. What convinced him that what he saw was a ghost is that he could see right through the head to the room behind the apparition. The head had dark hair and a full dark beard. It sounded much like the description of the molester that stood at the bottom of the basement stairs. The caretaker wondered if the paranormal investigation had something to do with this apparition. In his words, when asked what he looked like, he responded, "Well, it was only a head, but it had dark hair and a dark full beard. I don't know if the psychics stirred things up or why he was here and interested in what I was doing."

Before leaving, Victor commented that he felt sure one of the owners died in the house. During research, nothing turned up to validate that statement. Robert C. McKinney moved his family back to New York; Fannie died in Bloomington, Illinois; Dr. Walter Pater lived to be seventy-three years old and died in Hialeah, Florida, in 1969. The only death in the house that research shows is Bob Sherwin, who died in the parlor of the home he loved. However, that was fifteen years after Victor made the statement. But Victor is a psychic medium and clairvoyant. It could have been a premonition.

EPILOGUE

Do they really walk among us? Are we surrounded by the spirits of all who have passed on from this life? And, if we are interested, how do we find the ghosts of our ancestors in Hamilton, Ohio?

Often, when talking about ghost hunting, the communicating spirits and psychic impressions seem to be from the distant past. This book is no exception, as the accounts in this book have related to those who died long ago. That should be expected when your search takes you to historic areas, to houses that have existed for over one hundred years. It is much easier to immerse yourself in the past when the past is all around you.

But if people transition to spirit, there should certainly be some encounters with those who have recently passed. You don't have to be a professional medium to connect with your loved ones who are in spirit. Have you ever dreamed of the person who has died? Or maybe you have been in a dangerous situation and noticed the familiar smell of a loved one? Or it could be as simple as feeling their presence. The spirit of your loved one is with you, trying to let you know they are there.

There are ways that you can initiate that communication, but it takes practice. You need to change your focus and be present in the moment, concentrate on your breathing and release all the distractions that normally occupy your mind. Mastering meditation is a helpful way of closing out the physical world so you can focus on the spiritual. It might help if you immerse yourself in a place that your loved one would have occupied or surround yourself with the things that belonged to or had meaning to the person who passed. Hold their image in your mind and talk to them, ask questions without expecting an answer. And if you are able to establish a connection your response may come in the form of images or thoughts.

Of course, a simpler, less time-consuming effort would involve seeking out the support of a medium who has already developed this skill. The year 2021 ushers in the Age of Aquarius, a period that lasts for 2,160 years, on average. According to Corina Crysler, a transformational astrologer, "Aquarians channel from the collective consciousness and ether, and bring the intangible to life with their creations." And in this Age of Aquarius, as more people believe in a world beyond the physical, you can find an increased number of people who claim to be able to speak to the dead. They make a living by selling you on their ability to connect you with your loved one. But not all are genuine, so you want to spend the time to find a legitimate medium who has proven himself or herself. Do not be duped.

> [In the Age of Aquarius,] *the power is turning over to the individual, and giving the freedom for you to choose your own reality based on what aligns with your soul.*
>
> —*Adama Sesay, astrologer*

There is an abundance of mediums offering their skills, and their abilities are as varied as the personalities they bring to the table. The Dayton Lane Historic District took great care in selecting spiritualists to partner with the neighborhood. Other than the annual ghost walk, they have created an event that allows you to take advantage of the research they have done to locate the best mediums in our area.

DAYTON LANE HISTORIC DISTRICT GHOST WALK

Dayton Lane, like many old neighborhoods, had become run down from neglect over the years. But in 1972, it was lovingly brought back to life by Dr. Sherry Corbett, who in broad daylight was murdered in the neighborhood to which she devoted so much of her time. She and her partner Bob Sherwin ignited a renaissance in this beautiful old neighborhood, restoring the character of many of the homes, big and small.

Several neighbors were comfortably gathered around a fire after a successful Dayton Lane May Promenade. The sun had set, and talk turned to the history of the neighborhood that was slowly being revitalized by a younger generation moving in and taking back the neighborhood. It was during that cool spring evening that the ghost walk was conceived. The conversation about homes shown during the Promenade turned to talk about the strange occurrences in some of the houses. Unbelievable stories. In the days that followed, curiosity on the part of some of the neighbors led to a discussion about bringing in a psychic to see if there was any merit to the stories told around the firepit. Glowing embers took flight from the aged timber into the ever-darkening sky. Stars blinked on, and the ambiance of a mesmerizing flame lent credence to the possibility of truth to the many ghostly tales shared.

For centuries, people have lived, married, borne children and died in the ancestral homes lining the streets. Many believe those who have passed on are still strolling the streets and wandering through the houses. The Dayton Lane Ghost Walk annually shares the history and stories of unexplained phenomena occurring in its historic neighborhood over the years.

In 2003, the governing board of the district contracted a renowned psychic to explore the more supernaturally active homes in Dayton Lane. Those investigations were witnessed, videotaped and recorded by a few of the board members, and the results were documented. Some of the more significant findings were validated with research from materials found in the Cummins Local History Room at the downtown Lane Public Library, a building itself with a rich history. The Cummins Room was named after George C. Cummins (1903–1980), a prominent Hamilton attorney and active local historian. It contains myriad resources starting from the early years of Butler County, including newspapers on microfilm going back to the early years of the city. It was startling how accurate the impressions from the psychic proved to be. Some of those validated stories are included in this book.

The psychic readings and impressions from the homes that could be validated became the catalyst for what is known as the Dayton Lane Historic District Ghost Walk, which continues to be held annually. The neighborhood has homes both large and small, most of them with stories to tell. There was reluctance by some members of the Dayton Lane Board to host such an event; there was concern that living descendants might take offense, and some just thought it wouldn't generate enough interest to make it worthwhile. The event was advertised two weeks before the first tour. The news article did reach some who thought it best not to stir up the spirits of the ancestors, and the weekend before the first tour there was a self-described "Holy Ghost

The Wolf Gazebo in Campbell Avenue Park, the starting point for the annual Dayton Lane Ghost Walk. *Author's collection*.

Left: Guests gather round to hear tales of hauntings at "The Mill" as presented by Dr. Tom Nye. *Dr. Tom Nye, Dayton Lane Historic Area board member.*

Right: Annual ghost walk lantern-led tours begin in Campbell Avenue Park and continue through the streets of the Dayton Lane Historic District. *Dr. Tom Nye, Dayton Lane Historic Area board member.*

Walk." A group of people walked the neighborhood in protest and prayed for the people of the neighborhood who dared participate in the fundraiser. That was also written about in the paper and worked as the best advertising the district could possibly hope for. Over seven hundred guests attended, and the tours went long into the night. Subsequent years a limit was put on the number of people who could attend to make it more manageable.

The Dayton Lane Ghost Walk continues to take place annually in October, normally the weekend before Halloween, and begins at the Wolf Gazebo in Campbell Avenue Park.

The event takes place mostly outside, regardless of weather, rain or shine. Tours leave the gazebo on the half hour and stop at houses that have been read by Victor Paruta, researched and validated by the Dayton Lane Board members. The host shares the anomalies and the history of each place along the way where spirits have been found, and if a psychic is on the tour, he or she gives their personal psychic impressions. The tour ends at a reception house, where refreshments are complimentary. Normally, one to five psychics are present at the reception to offer private readings for those who want them. It's a night of entertainment that's very much worth the price of the ticket.

The walk is a fundraiser, so there is a small ticket price, which includes a lantern-led tour and hors d'oeuvres at a reception in one of the mansions. Information regarding the current events will be advertised on the Hamilton's Dayton Lane Facebook Page, with tickets available on Eventbrite.

A Psychic Evening and Reading–Dayton Lane Spirit Circles

Some years there have been reenactors playing the souls who have passed, and some years the ghost walk event uses psychic mediums to lead the tours through the neighborhood in combination with a historian. Recently, a second night has been added to the event and a group of mediums host spirit circles where you can connect with your loved ones who have crossed into spirit.

Mediums can vary in their skills, and some may display more than one ability. Most think of mediums as being clairvoyant, meaning they have the ability to "see" beyond the range of ordinary perception, sometimes with visions or merely images. Some have the gift of clairaudience, which gives them the faculty to "hear" what is inaudible.

A physical medium can include a trance medium where the spirit speaks through the medium, but it would also include a medium who takes on the characteristics of the spirit they are communicating with. In the past, the Spirit Circles have included all of these with the exception of trance mediumship. Reservations are required for that event, and it sells out quickly.

Dayton Lane has assembled a talented pool of mediums who, for the first half of the event, conduct evidential platform readings. A skill developed along the path of becoming a certified medium, evidential readings give the audience evidence of the spirit communication by describing physical attributes, personality characteristics or something that provides enough clues that someone present can identify with the spirit coming through. This event has brought some great joy and hope that their loved one continues on after death, and it has reduced some participants to tears. It can be emotional depending on the circumstances of the person getting the message.

Midway through the event, the crowd breaks into smaller groups and works individually with one of the mediums. The circle consists of five

Victor Paruta is giving platform readings for guests who gathered to participate in Spirit Circles at the McKinney Mansion. *Author's collection.*

or six participants and a medium who gives each person a five-minute communication from someone in their life who has passed over.

This is a popular event and typically sells out within twenty-four hours.

GERMAN VILLAGE

Several locations in Hamilton's Historic German Village provide opportunities for the curious to delve into the paranormal. Periodically, the Butler County Historical Society, located at 327 North Second Street, hosts paranormal investigation events that are open to the public for the price of a ticket. However, these events only accommodate a limited number of people. The investigators have specialized equipment that offers a heightened experience for the guest. Another option is to make an appointment with Kathy Creighton, the director, to tour the museum. You may experience your own "visitations."

The Butler County Historical Society is located in the John Benninghofen house on North Second Street. *Author's collection.*

The home base for the World's Largest Ghost Hunt is in German Village in Hamilton, Ohio. This epic event takes place on the official National Ghost Hunting Day. Simultaneously taking place all around the world, this event draws thousands internationally to the spirit-seeking experience. Ghost hunters from all over the world join forces on the same day and time, making allowances for different time zones of course, to connect with those who have passed over in historic properties. Taking place every year in September, it is open for the public to participate. In 2019, the hunt encompassed seven countries and was controlled from several German Village historic properties, the Butler County Historical Society on North Second Street, the German Village Carriage House and the Soldiers and Sailors Monument in downtown Hamilton. People from around the world can follow the investigations via live streams. This global event always takes place on the last Saturday in September. The 2019 hunt was featured on the *Today* show and on the Third Hour of Today, demonstrating communications using unattended flashlights for yes/no answers to questions. The core purpose of this event centers on community service to historic preservation. Plus, it increases public awareness for

The Historic Butler County Courthouse is located in downtown Hamilton just a block from the bridge. *Author's collection.*

parapsychology studies and traditional techniques in evidence gathering. The control center in Hamilton allows the attendees to observe the volunteers as they track activity from around the world, which in 2020 included the countries of Australia, Canada, New Zealand, Great Britain and many cities and states in the United States.

Downtown Hamilton

The Butler County Courthouse does not have a formal tour at the time of this writing, and to enter the beautiful historic building you are required to pass through a metal detector. If you have the opportunity to tour the building, you may run into a ghostly night watchman who was killed during a robbery in the 1860s who wanders the halls. His attackers killed him using ether before hanging him to make it look like a suicide. He is said to have materialized in front of employees and made the clock chime twenty-one times. During the historic 1913 flood, when approximately one hundred people died after ten to eighteen feet of water flowed into residential neighborhoods, the basement of the courthouse became a temporary morgue. Who knows what is hiding in the shadows of the basement?

Butler County Fairgrounds

The Butler County Fairgrounds has played an important role in multiple ways that could introduce you to the paranormal, and to this day it is used in ways other than the Butler County Fair. It lies along Erie Highway with entry at Fairgrove Avenue. Prior to the Civil War, this was the original home of Camp Hamilton, where the city's soldiers were trained for battle during the Civil War. Following the war, the grounds were used for traveling circuses that came to town, and it provided a perfect venue for the Wild West shows of Pawnee Bill and then Buffalo Bill Cody's reenactments. You might be there for the county fair or one of the many other events that take place on the fifty-four acres that encompass a large number of exhibition buildings and a large grandstand. There you can watch monster trucks, tractor pulls, rodeos, even the circus. If you happen to be at the fairgrounds, make a point of walking around the grandstand and the surrounding area. You just may run into the restless soul of the man who roams the area beneath and around the arena. He has been seen outside the entrance to the grandstand with blood dripping from the wound in his head. Reportedly, he shot himself in one of the public restrooms. Is this a true story, or just an urban legend? Visit the Butler County Fairgrounds and decide for yourself.

BIBLIOGRAPHY

Amadeo, Kimberly. "What Was Deinstitutionalization?" The Balance. https://www.thebalance.com/deinstitutionalization-3306067.

BBC. "Religions—Spiritualism: History of Modern Spiritualism." https://www.bbc.co.uk/religion/religions/spiritualism/history/history.shtml.

Blount, Jim. "Opera House Was Show Business Center." *Journal News*, November 1, 1995. sites.google.com/a/lanepl.org/jbcols/1995/november.

———. "Well-Known Butler County Men Defied Lincoln." *Journal News*, October 2, 2002. sites.google.com/a/lanepl.org/jbcols/2002/october.

Burzynski, Amy. "Hamilton Is Home Base for World's Largest Ghost Hunt." *Springfield News Sun*, August 27, 2018. www.springfieldnewssun.com/news/local/hamilton-home-base-for-world-largest-ghost-hunt/LvntAUpQeXkVvC8B0XFyKL/.

Butler County Democrat. "Columbia Plant Sold to O.M. Bake for $42,000." December 14, 1911.

Civil War Talk. "Hamilton, Ohio Horse Rehabilitation Camp Site." civilwartalk.com/threads/hamilton-ohio-horse-rehabilitation-camp-site.160091/.

Clark, Michael D. "Hamilton City Arts Icon Passes." *Enquirer*, May 4 2014. www.cincinnati.com/story/news/history/lives-remembered/2014/05/04/hamilton-city-arts-icon-passes/8628503/.

Coughlin, Sara. "Why Kids Always Claim To See 'Ghosts.'" Refinery29. www.refinery29.com/en-us/2018/10/213091/kids-who-see-ghosts.

Creekbaum, Chelle. "TriOPs Team Invites Locals to Explore Haunted Hamilton Restaurant." *Journal News*, September 9, 2011. www.journal-news.com/news/local/triops-team-invites-locals-explore-haunted-hamilton-restaurant/Cw9EOTgW3W0c0j2RgjuqHJ/.

Daily News Journal (Hamilton, OH). "Mrs. Belle Andrews, 81, Taken by Death." September 20, 1937.

Edgar Cayce's A.R.E. "Who Was Edgar Cayce?" www.edgarcayce.org/edgar-cayce/his-life/.

Encyclopedia.com. "History of the United States and Canada North American Indigenous Peoples Miami Indians." www.encyclopedia.com/history/united-states-and-canada/north-american-indigenous-peoples/miami-indians.

Facebook. "Hamiltucky Paranormal Investigations." www.facebook.com/HamiltuckyParanormal/.

———. "Spiritual Realm Paranormal." www.facebook.com/Spiritualrealmparanormal/.

Gambony, Gina. "Communique: EXPO 216 Presents 'Evidential Mediumship Demonstration': Death & Dying." WHQR. www.whqr.org/post/communique-expo-216-presents-evidential-mediumship-demonstration-death-dying#stream/0.

Garis, Mary Grace. "2021 Heralds the New Age of Aquarius—Here's What 5 Astrologers Want You to Know About It." Well+Good, www.wellandgood.com/what-is-age-aquarius/.

Gendisasters. "Hamilton, OH Courthouse Fire, Mar 1912—Courthouse Destroyed." http://www.gendisasters.com/ohio/13395/hamilton-oh-court-house-fire-mar-1912.

Hamilton Daily News. "Confers With Sheriff Who Objects to 'Those All-Night Affairs'—Epperson Reports Residents of Vicinity Aroused." July 23, 1925.

———. "Miami Valley Spiritualist Church." April 2, 1927.

Hamilton Daily News Journal. "Dr. Keely, Prominent Dentist, Dead." November 1, 1934.

Hamilton Evening Democrat. "Children's Party." June 27, 1901.

———. "Dr. Wayne to Give a Spiritualistic Séance at the Jefferson Theater." November 25, 1903.

Ingle, Sheila. "Riding the Rails During the Great Depression." sheilaingle.com/2017/05/01/riding-the-rails-during-the-great-depression/.

Johnson, Karin. "Do the Undead Roam Halls of Butler County Historical Society?" WLWT, October 31, 2019. www.wlwt.com/article/do-the-the-undead-roam-halls-of-butler-county-historical-society/29658239.

————. "Paranormal Group Says Hamilton Law Office Is Haunted." WLWT, October 4, 2017. www.wlwt.com/article/paranormal-group-says-hamilton-law-office-is-haunted-3/3528760.

Kiesewetter, Sue. "Butler County Fair Runs July 21–27 at Fairgrounds in Hamilton." *Cincinnati Enquirer*, July 18, 2019. www.cincinnati.com/story/news/2019/07/18/butler-county-fair-runs-july-21-27-fairgrounds-hamilton/1767381001/.

McKenzie & Snyder, Attorneys at Law. "Haunted Houses Cast Spooky Shadow Over Hamilton, OH." mckenzie-snyder.com/haunted-houses-cast-spooky-shadow-over-hamilton-oh.

————. "229 Dayton Street Is 'Haunted.'" mckenzie-snyder.com/229-dayton-street-haunted.

Midwestern Regional Climate Center. "The Great Flood of 1913 100 Years Later." mrcc.illinois.edu/1913Flood/communities/hamilton.shtml.

Moore, Anna. "What Is It about Kids and Ghosts? Anna Moore Hears the Tales That Will Send Shivers Down Your Spine." *Daily Mail*, January 25, 2020. www.dailymail.co.uk/home/you/article-7891245/What-kids-ghosts-Anna-Moore-hears-tales-send-shivers-spine.html.

National Ghost Hunting Day. "World's Largest Ghost Hunting Event." nationalghosthuntingday.com/the-hunt.

Ohio Exploration Society. "Butler County Hauntings & Legends." www.ohioexploration.com/paranormal/hauntings/butlercounty/.

Ohio History Connection. "Weyapiersenwah." ohiohistorycentral.org/w/Weyapiersenwah.

Paruta, Victor. victorparuta.com.

Quackenbush, Jannette Rae. *Ohio Ghost Hunter Guide V: A Haunted Hocking Ghost Hunter Guide*. Hocking Hills, OH: 21 Crows Dusk to Dawn Publishing, 2013.

Report, Staff. "Are There Ghosts in Hamilton's Benninghofen House? Here's Your Chance to Find Out." *Journal News*, October 16, 2018. www.journal-news.com/news/are-there-ghosts-hamilton-benninghofen-house-here-your-chance-find-out/z7xJDqwouN126GHlqBVHrJ/.

Republican (Hamilton, OH). "Impaled on a Fence." August 16, 1894.

Robinette, Eric. "Ryan's Tavern Hosts 'Spirited' Tours Led by Hamilton Paranormal Group." *Journal News*, October 27, 2010. www.journal-news.com/lifestyles/holiday/ryan-tavern-hosts-spirited-tours-led-hamilton-paranormal-group/r3yYqfphJBB7TG4kPMUfuO/.

Robson, David. "Psychology: The Truth About the Paranormal." In Depth: Psychology, BBC. October 30, 2014. www.bbc.com/future/ article/20141030-the-truth-about-the-paranormal.

Rutledge, Mike. "NBC's 'Today Show' Came to Butler County for a Ghost Hunting Segment. Then They Heard Noises." *Journal News*, October 28, 2019. www.journal-news.com/lifestyles/holiday/nbc-today-show-came-butler-county-for-ghost-hunting-segment-then-they-heard-noises/ fGwOrAwUNHWYes268wbekN/.

———. "'This Is a Very Haunted Building': NBC Comes to Hamilton for Segment on Worldwide Ghost Hunt." *Dayton Daily News*, November 25, 2019. www.daytondailynews.com/news/local/this-very-haunted-building-nbc-comes-hamilton-for-segment-worldwide-ghost-hunt/ v5i03Ro2ABLNikEQITMA7H/.

———. "'World's Largest Ghost Hunt' Happening Saturday in Hamilton: What to Know." *Journal News*, September 27, 2019. www.journal-news.com/news/local/world-largest-ghost-hunt-happening-saturday-hamilton-what-know/5yUg5gkrksMnNvgDUyD0LJ/.

Schmidt, Maria Pons. "Haunted Journeys Home Page." Haunted Journeys. www.hauntedjourneys.com/index.php.

Seppi, Antony. "Walking Tours of Historic Hamilton, Ohio." Greater Hamilton Convention and Visitors Bureau. issuu.com/antonyseppi/ docs/walking_tours_brochure-unsecure.

Stander, Thomas F. "Camp Hamilton—Butler County Civil War 150." Butler County Sesquicentennial Committee. sites.google.com/site/ butlercountycw150/bc-civil-war-history/the-places/camp-hamilton.

The Walking Tour Company. "Haunted Sites in Hamilton. www. thewalkingtourcompany.com/in-depth---haunted-all.html.

Wikipedia. "Butler County Courthouse (Ohio)." https://en.wikipedia.org/ wiki/Butler_County_Courthouse_(Ohio).

INDEX

ABOUT THE AUTHOR

Shi O'Neill is a retired teacher and an avid reader who loves to immerse herself in a good story. She lives in a close-knit historic neighborhood in a small Ohio town that serves as her inspiration. Her first work, a novel, was based on her experiences in this historic district where she has lived for a quarter of a century. She serves on multiple historic boards, which augments her love of local history. She raised two beautiful children and has lived with her loving husband for the last twenty-five years in a nineteenth-century three-story mansion. Although Shi has been writing for many years just for the love of it, she is now publishing her work.

Visit us at
www.historypress.com

www.ingramcontent.com/pod-product-compliance
Lightning Source LLC
Chambersburg PA
CBHW070348100426
42812CB00005B/1454